"What makes a good teacher... not what you do, but what you inspire others to do. Whether you are a public or private school leader, teacher or parent looking to actively engage in your child's learning journey, this book clearly identifies the conditions needed to create independent thinkers who are ready to take on the world."

—Christy Todd, 2024 National Teacher of the Year Finalist, 2024 Georgia Teacher of the Year

"There is no shortage of educational leadership books on the market today. What surprised me about *The Playbook for Self-Directed Learning* is its focus on learners rather than teachers. Thigpen, Collier, Bryant, and Toles challenge school leaders to rebel against what is considered best practice by allowing—more importantly demanding—that students be given the opportunity to struggle, fail, reflect, and try again. It has been 30 years since I've read a book that embraces a constructivist theory of teaching and learning and provides the reader with a roadmap for transforming schools from adult- to child-centered. This is a must-read for educators and parents who want schools that simultaneously focus on academic achievement, character formation, and creativity."

—Beth Purvis, EdD, Former Secretary of Education, State of Illinois, and CEO, Chicago International Charter School

"What if young people could follow their passions, design their learning, and organize their schooling in ways that helped them flourish as humans and as citizens? In this book, experienced educators who are national leaders in the field of self-directed learning offer us a soup-to-nuts guide in how to make this dream a reality. Chockful of examples, suffused with wisdom, and forthright about challenges, this hopeful yet practical book shows us both why and how students can be put in charge of their own learning. A must read for anyone who wants to transform industrial model schools into places of purpose and passion for both students and adults."

—Jal Mehta, Professor of Education, Harvard Graduate School of Education

"The *Playbook for Self-Directed Learning* is THE tool every educator needs to raise up future-ready learners. Fostering motivated, independent, and creative thinkers is not just beneficial, it is essential in our increasingly interconnected world. This book will guide you through creating a self-directed learning environment that equips students with the agency and confidence needed to navigate any endeavor they pursue. Whether you're an educator, parent, or simply curious about the future of education, this book is a must-read."

—Allison K. Cochran, Ed.S, Educational Technology Coach, Lambert High School, Forsyth County Public Schools

"As someone who will soon be designing a new school from the ground up, this is the book I've been waiting on. The Playbook for Self-Directed Learning not only gives *me* the language, frameworks, and case studies to better understand what I want, but also the opportunity to share this Playbook with partners and staff to nurture a shared vision from the get-go. My biggest takeaway is that fostering student agency won't always be easy— but it will always be worth it. In a nutshell, that's life … and that's what we should be preparing learners for, after all."

—Dr. Ali Imad Fadlallah, author, *March Forth: From The Prison of Minds*

"At a moment of massive social, political, and physical climate change, it's difficult to predict what the future will look like. However, if one thing is for certain, it's critical we prepare our next generation of humans to navigate it with commitment, confidence and purpose. In this book, Thigpen, Collier, Bryant, and Toles lay out a comprehensive, practical, and realistic vision for creating schools where doing this is at the core of teaching and learning. Importantly, this book isn't a theoretical call to action or a general provocation. Rather, it's a playbook for every educator, in every kind of school, addressing head on the very real constraints educators might face as they try to bring self-directed learning to life in their own context. It offers clear and doable strategies and techniques for navigating barriers and enacting a compelling vision and driving real change at a moment when our kids need and deserve it the most."

—Dr. Beth Rabbitt, Ed.L.D. Chief Executive Officer,
The Learning Accelerator

"Finally! And not a moment too soon, *The Playbook for Self-Directed Learning* is the book we need, and our children deserve. This essential guide is for every educator yearning to fulfill their calling and create learning environments that inspire and empower. Packed with practical strategies that can be implemented immediately, this book will reignite your passion for teaching and equip you with the tools to nurture students into the leaders and innovators they are destined to become. Our future depends on it."

—Mike Duncan, Ed.D., President & CEO,
Battelle for Kids

"I am excited to endorse *The Playbook for Self-Directed Learning* by Dr. Tyler Thigpen, Dr. Caleb Collier, Amber

Bryant, and Brittney Toles. This guide offers transformative strategies for fostering student agency and self-direction, essential for today's evolving educational landscape. By emphasizing the importance of supportive relationships, student choice, and purposeful struggle, this book equips educators with the tools to create environments where students can take charge of their learning and develop the skills needed for lifelong success. The detailed techniques and real-world examples make it an invaluable resource for anyone committed to transforming education and promoting student agency."
—Caroline Vander Ark, CEO, Getting Smart Collective

"The Playbook for Self-Directed Learning is a terrific, concrete, and practical guide for implementing the kinds of bold changes we need for young people to have real agency in their learning. The authors draw on their deep experience in creating thoughtfully designed learning environments that cultivate agency and self-direction to offer a powerful vision for self-directed learning, backed by concrete strategies and real-world examples. What sets this book apart is its unwavering focus on student agency. The authors convincingly argue that by empowering students to take ownership of their learning, we cultivate not only academic success but also the development of critical life skills like problem-solving, resilience, and a sense of purpose. Our education system needs more spaces where young people are empowered to fully realize their potential so that they can thrive in their future and this book provides a compelling and realistic roadmap for leaders in getting there."
—Kim Smith, Founder and CEO, LearnerStudio

"The Playbook for Self-Directed Learning pushed me to remember why I got into education in the first place and

what education can look like. I get caught up in the current state of education so much that I forget what education can be for students and for all of us! The Playbook not only provides helpful and concrete guidance; it also casts a vision for what we wish education could be for all of our students. And it's not just a wish--it can be a reality as evidenced in the Playbook!"
—Kentaro Iwasaki, Founder, Concentric Math; Co-Chair, Harvard Data Wise Network

"Now more than ever, we need to help learners take charge of their own educational journeys. But to do that, we must transform schooling. This book provides an outstanding resource for doing just that. The authors draw from their own experiences building and leading innovative learning environments and share practical tools and resources. A vital read for educators, administrators, parents, and, yes, students!"
—Jeff Wetzler, co-founder and board member, Transcend; former Chief Learning Officer, Teach For America; co-author, *Extraordinary Learning for All: How Communities Design Schools Where Everyone Thrives*; and author, *Ask: Tap Into the Hidden Wisdom of People Around You*

"The *Playbook for Self-Directed Learning* is an incredibly useful tool for any school leader or educator. It's brimming with practical techniques for leaders looking to cultivate learner agency. I highly recommend it for anyone looking to develop self-motivated learners and for educators looking to boost student engagement in their classrooms."
—Kimberly Dow, Executive Director, Khan Lab School

"*The Playbook for Self-Directed Learning* by Dr. Tyler Thigpen, Dr. Caleb Collier, Amber Bryant, and Brittney

Toles is a transformative guide for educators, leaders, parents, or anyone aiming to revolutionize the way we approach education. This book provides a comprehensive research-grounded and practical roadmap for facilitating and sustaining self-directed learning environments that foster students' agency, inquisitiveness, and lifelong learning. A perfect balance of lived, hands-on experiences, case studies, research, and theory, *The Playbook for Self-Directed Learning* is an accessible resource that can be leveraged by schools, families, teacher preparation programs, and even policy makers. It is a call to action to rethink and reshape our educational systems and practices, and provides the actionable steps, as well as the conversational and motivational tone necessary to fuel a powerful movement."

—Brandi B. Kenner, Ph.D, Founder & CEO, Choice-filled Lives Network; Malcolm Knowles Self-Directed Learning Lifetime Achievement Award Winner, International Society for Self-Directed Learning

"The Playbook for Self-Directed Learning" is a practitioner's best friend packed with easy-to-operationalize actions. Many are deceptively small shifts that offer promise to kickstart deeper change toward relevant, meaningful, empowering learning for every young person. This playbook illuminates multiple on-ramps for behaving your way into nurturing not only student agency, but deeper educator and parent confidence on the road to becoming facilitators of transformative deep learning."

—Dr. Leslie Bussey, CEO and Executive Director, Georgia Leadership Institute for School Improvement

"In a time of growing disenchantment with rote schooling and a one-size-fits-all approach to education, *The Playbook for Self-Directed Learning: A Leader's Guide to*

School Transformation and Student Agency by Dr. Tyler Thigpen, Dr. Caleb Collier, Amber Bryant, and Brittney Toles offers a refreshing and practical roadmap towards a different future. This isn't a theoretical treatise, but a hands-on guide for educators, administrators, and even parents, outlining a path towards self-directed learning for young people. While many discussions engage in the theoretical and what ought to be, *The Playbook* gives us a practical way forward, focusing on how to make learning empowering, meaningful, and practical for young people. The authors don't shy away from the challenges of self-direction and, while acknowledging the constraints of numerous systems of education and the need for a culture shift within schools and learning environments, they provide clear steps and inspiring real-world examples for how the positive shifts can actually be accomplished. The book empowers adults to create spaces where students take ownership of their learning journeys and embark on transformative experiences. *The Playbook for Self-Directed Learning* provides a compelling vision for learning that nurtures curiosity, critical thinking, and a lifelong love of learning. This is a must-read for anyone who believes in the transformative power of education and wants to take action."

—Dr. Babak Mostaghimi, founding partner, LearnerStudio; former Assistant Superintendent, Gwinnett County Public Schools, Georgia

"This is the book I needed as an educator and parent! Our future depends on raising self-directed learners, but our schools (and many of our parenting books) not only fail to provide an opportunity, but often work against self-directed learning. Tyler, Amber, Caleb, and Brittney have done a fantastic job of providing a detailed description of both the philosophy and practice of self-directed learning. I look forward to re-visiting many of its chapters as I continue my own journey as a parent of adults, educational consultant, and (hopefully) future grandparent. Life just got a little more glorious."

—Dr. Jason Lustig Yamashiro, retired northern California superintendent; parent of three; and founder, Joyful Learning Network

"*The Playbook for Self-Directed Learning* is an essential read for anyone committed to empowering kids through education. With a relentless focus on the needs of children, this book transcends constraints, offering actionable insights and clear purposes. It masterfully breaks down the complexities of fostering self-directed learning, providing a comprehensive framework that ensures every reader can grasp the 'why' and 'how.' An invaluable resource for creating meaningful educational opportunities, it is a beacon of hope and practical guidance in the evolving landscape of learning."

—Nikolaus Namba, Managing Partner, Transcend; former Director, 21st Century Learning at Lindsay Unified School District; former Chief Academic Officer, Ingenium Schools; co-editor, *Beyond Reform: Systemic Shifts Toward Personalized Learning*

"As a San Francisco public school system leader, I remember having a conversation with Dr. Richard Elmore years ago about coherence and capacity building in PK-12 school systems. When I asked him what he was *really* excited to see in the future of teaching and learning in all classrooms, he paused, then shared the following paraphrased thoughts, "Students should be engaged, involved, and in charge of their learning with an ability to monitor their own progress and provide input on learning design. They should be cognizant of learning objectives and work towards meeting those goals in meaningful, relevant ways. They should be able to move around and access vital resources while learning. Teachers should be facilitators of learning, working alongside students." What does this really look like in schools? This *Playbook* shows us practical ways to increase student agency and transform schools through learner-led spaces while centering equity and excellence. Highly recommend it!!"

—Dr. Bonnie Lo, Harvard Graduate School of Education (Education Consultant, Teaching Team Member & Research Design) and PK-12 School Systems Administrator

"For those seeking ways to empower children to find their voice, nurture their individuality, and motivate them to become independent thinkers and decision-makers, this book is a valuable resource. Rooted in research-based techniques, it provides a toolbox of strategies to increase student-directed learning as educational methods continue to evolve. The impact of COVID was a wake-up to both parents and educators and prompted a renewed focus on the current educational model. This book serves as a call to action, outlining strategies to empower students toward self-directed learning. This book is clear, concise, and easy to read. It discusses the development of learners and meeting them where they are, building supportive relationships with all stakeholders- including their peers and shedding light on their purpose in life being bigger than themselves."

—Sharon Reddick, M.Ed., Early Childhood Education; former public school administrator, Gwinnett County, Georgia

The Playbook for Self-Directed Learning

The Playbook for Self-Directed Learning offers school leaders a student-centered, relationship-driven approach to fostering learner-led success and autonomy at school. In self-directed learning, learners set their own goals, manage their own progress, and assess their own outcomes, all under the guidance of teachers and administrators. This accessible book offers evidence-based insights, real-world examples, and practical techniques for leaders seeking to transform their schools and empower students to become responsible for their own learning within an interdependent network of relationships with educators, peers, and involved adults. Each chapter includes a variety of strategies for supporting the conditions in which students can enthusiastically develop self-regulation, time management, adaptability, problem-solving, and other important skills. Principals, superintendents, teacher-leaders, and curriculum/assessment designers will come away with bold, yet intuitive methods for transforming schools into self-directed learning environments.

Dr. Tyler S. Thigpen is Head of Schools of The Forest School: An Acton Academy in Fayetteville, Georgia, Co-Founder and Executive Director of the Institute for Self-Directed Learning, Guest Lecturer at Harvard University's Graduate School of Education, and Academic Director at the University of Pennsylvania Graduate School of Education.

Dr. Caleb Collier is Co-Founder of The Forest School: An Acton Academy in Fayetteville, Georgia, and Director and Head of Research at the Institute for Self-Directed Learning.

Amber Bryant is Assistant Head of School for Learning at The Forest School: An Acton Academy in Fayetteville, Georgia, and Co-Founder of The Forest School and Institute for Self-Directed Learning.

Brittney Toles is Co-Founder, High School Guide, and Assistant Head of School for Culture and Enrichment of The Forest School: An Acton Academy in Fayetteville, Georgia, and Co-Founder of the Institute for Self-Directed Learning.

The Playbook for Self-Directed Learning

A Leader's Guide
to School Transformation
and Student Agency

Tyler S. Thigpen, Caleb Collier, Amber Bryant,
and Brittney Toles

Routledge
Taylor & Francis Group

NEW YORK AND LONDON

Designed cover image: Tyler Thigpen

First published 2025
by Routledge
605 Third Avenue, New York, NY 10158

and by Routledge
4 Park Square, Milton Park, Abingdon, Oxon, OX14 4RN

Routledge is an imprint of the Taylor & Francis Group, an informa business

© 2025 Tyler S. Thigpen, Caleb Collier, Amber Bryant, and Brittney Toles

The right of Tyler S. Thigpen, Caleb Collier, Amber Bryant, and Brittney Toles to be identified as authors of this work has been asserted in accordance with sections 77 and 78 of the Copyright, Designs and Patents Act 1988.

ISBN: 978-1-032-78955-2 (hbk)
ISBN: 978-1-032-75887-9 (pbk)
ISBN: 978-1-003-48989-4 (ebk)

DOI: 10.4324/9781003489894

Typeset in Palatino
by SPi Technologies India Pvt Ltd (Straive)

Contents

1

The What and Why of Self-Directed Learning

An Introduction

We get it. If you're picking up this book, then you're probably a busy leader who cares a ton about kids. We get it because we, too, have been there and are still in it. We—Amber, Brittney, Caleb, and Tyler—lead a small, self-directed, diverse-by-design, purpose-focused, character-forging school in Trilith, Georgia, south of Atlanta. We have also worked with hundreds of public and private school leaders who want to build better schools. We're parents who care deeply about our kids' education. We have skin in the game, you might say, having our own children at our school. As two white men and two black women who have worked together for six years, we also appreciate what it's like to bring different perspectives. We have learned to collaborate across lines of difference, to help a community learn to live together, and to use culturally appropriate techniques that we, our staff, and (we believe) others can use to empower the next generation.

DOI: 10.4324/9781003489894-1

In this book, we're going to argue for an approach we call self-directed learning (which we'll define shortly). Colleagues elsewhere use terms like student agency, learner-led, learner-driven, self-determined, and learner-centered. While there are nuanced differences, we've found more similarities—and solidarity—in our collective quest to keep students motivated and equipped as they build self-leadership and purpose-seeking skills that eventually translate into the betterment of those around them. We're less interested in terms, camps, and divisions. We're way more interested in unity when it comes to what's best for kids.

One thing is certain: the world needs self-directed problem solvers. The half-life of knowledge will continue to shrink. AI-driven technologies continue to grow at a rapid pace. The understandings of the competencies a graduate will need to demonstrate in the next five or ten years will be ever-evolving. One thing that will remain the same, though, is that young people will need the skills to be adaptable to a constantly changing world. See this book as an invitation to you and your education team to experiment, tinker, and grow in your own abilities to cultivate self-directed learners.

Leading schools is hard. It takes courage and unbelievably thick skin. Your time is precious. We don't want to waste it. So, we'll start with the end in mind. We'll tell you up front where we're going with this book. Here are the five main points that we want to get across, and that we hope you'll consider as you read:

1. **The designs of most schools and classrooms today disempower children by shutting out or shutting down their feelings, thoughts, and plans**. This is a tragedy. The longer children live, move, and have their being in environments where they're regularly told what to do and what to learn, the more they become dependent on others. We believe teachers, school leaders, parents, and caregivers have good hearts and want students to have vibrant futures. However, the design of most schools and

classrooms has the opposite effect. The COVID-19 pandemic provided an insight into this dependency. In an instant, when learning went remote, we could see clearly just how many students across our nation were dependent on others, waiting around on others to engage them and tell them what to learn and what to do. This reality isn't just detrimental for schools, it's detrimental for our world. We need to be graduating young adults who have purpose-seeking skills, who aspire to help others, and who have learned how to learn. In this book, we'll talk about the journey of leading school transformation. We'll include concrete steps your community can take to get unstuck and move towards a world where students have maximum ownership of their education.

2. **Surrounding children with supportive relationships and giving them as much choice, voice, and autonomy as possible throughout their learning journey will give them the best chance at finding a purpose in life bigger than themselves and ultimately living the kinds of lives they want to live**. Early in this book, we will try and back up this claim with research, existing practices, testimonies, and proof points from schools and classrooms. We won't go in depth with research. We will give you the highlights and tell you where else to look if you want to go deeper. We will go super in depth on this next point.

3. **Self-directed learning is possible in a public, standards-based environment where resources are lacking, barriers are many, and constraints are real, as well as in a private school environment where parental college acceptance expectations are high**. To that end, there are many and varied *techniques* that school leaders, teachers, and parents and caregivers can use to support and motivate children to take even more charge of their learning just as soon as they're put into practice. These techniques are achievable now regardless of whether you're in district

schools, charter schools, private schools, homeschools, or out-of-school learning environments. This book includes almost every technique we've ever seen or used. As such, we hope this book becomes a kind of playbook for you and your team. We hope you mark all over it, try things out, and have professional development discussions or trainings about the techniques in this book.

4. **When school leaders, teachers, and parents and caregivers are aligned in motivating and supporting children to direct their own learning, then their development will accelerate.** If those stakeholder groups are not aligned, then children's development will be slowed. In this book, we argue that the two most important things school leaders should do are 1) to surround children with many and deep caring, supportive relationships and 2) to get all stakeholders rowing in the same direction when it comes to the level of autonomy and workload students are responsible for and thus what they can achieve. Please hear us—if children get mixed messages from the caring adults in their lives about what they can and cannot do, then children will not be as empowered as they could be.

5. **Finally, children need, and benefit tremendously from, productive struggle.** When rightly supported and motivated, children can direct their own learning. When they experience the natural consequences of their choices—both good and bad—in the context of a supportive community, then they learn and develop in significant ways. For decades in American education, we've considered it a noble cause to try and meet the needs of all children. It's not noble. Children need affirmation, attention, comfort, and affection, yes. But they also need to struggle when learning something new and making life choices. We're not talking about panic or lack of safety. We're talking about letting children experience right-sized challenges.

In this book, we'll show what it's like for educators to "let go" in responsible, caring ways so that students' abilities can blossom and their character can grow.

Our book is different from great books on school leadership available now. For example, Mary Moss Brown's and Alisa Berger's (2014) book *The Essential Guide to Fearless School Leaders* illuminates four levers of change—curriculum, culture, time, and human capital—to advance innovation. Our book agrees but focuses on how these levers can be used to achieve greater self-direction. Doug Lemov's (2021) *Teach Like a Champion* helped a movement of educators and leaders with techniques aimed at focusing students' attention on learning standards no matter what. Unlike Lemov's, our book offers techniques that maximize time, space, and autonomy for students to express and develop their feelings, thoughts, and plans. *The Self-Driven Child* by William Stixrud and Ned Johnson (2018) shares strategies for adults to foster a sense of control and autonomy in children. Our work adds strategies for learners and leaders and includes a range of tactics that can be applied across an entire school model, from curriculum to roles to operations to community practices and more.

The book in your hands now includes but also transcends an emphasis on academics. We respect standards and direct instruction, and we'll show you how self-direction can happen even in a teacher-centric, standards-based environment. But learning math, science, history, and English isn't the main point. Leading humane schools where students flourish, learn to learn, find purpose, and help others is our top priority. The techniques we outline in the book will push you and your staff to "let go" more than ever. The more you implement from this book, the more push back you'll get, yes. Change is hard. But you'll also see positive changes in students—and in a short amount of time. Down the road, graduates of all stripes will reach out and thank you for the productive struggle you facilitated for them.

So that you can know as a leader how to implement any changes, we've organized the techniques into the main components of schooling over which most of you have some degree of control or influence. These are they system elements of any school:

1. Vision/School Concept
2. Curriculum, Pedagogy, and Assessment
3. Schedule and Routines
4. Roles, Development, and Management Model
5. Community Practices and School Culture
6. Bridges and Partnerships
7. Tech and Tech Infrastructure
8. Continuous Learning and Improvement Mechanisms
9. Space and Facilities
10. Budget, Operations, and Logistics
11. Admissions
12. Communication

Each time we name a technique, we'll tell you the category of innovation it is so that you know where in your mind—and your school's design—to place it. We'll also give you a sense of the ripple effects each technique will have in your school system (across other system elements). This will help you train your team, find resources, and manage expectations with stakeholders.

Lastly, because you're busy, we've tried to keep the book dense and digestible, and not to belabor the points. We'll get straight to it. So, here we go.

A Case for Change

Imagine three photographs of a classroom. One from a hundred years ago. Another from fifty years ago. And the third taken just this week. Some features of the classrooms will be different, like updated furniture, decor, and technology. But many elements of the photos would be consistent. Kids, sitting passively in desks, arranged in rows and facing the same direction. A teacher standing or sitting at the front managing the delivery of the content. Not much has changed in the traditional design of school over the past century.

It's a sad fact that most students spend their days sitting in their seats, listening to adults answer questions they didn't ask and following rules that they didn't make. What does spending years in that environment do to a young person? How does it impact their own thoughts, ideas, and plans for their lives?

This approach to schooling has led to an epidemic of what Zaretta Hammond calls "dependent learners." Dependent learners, "struggle because we don't offer them sufficient opportunities in the classroom to develop the cognitive skills and habits of mind that would prepare them to take on the more advanced academic tasks" (Hammond, 2014). This epidemic has been raging for decades, but it took the arrival of a global pandemic—the COVID-19 outbreak—to really uncover how dependent our students are on the structures of school (teachers, schedules, etc.). Without a teacher in the room to tell them what to do, many students spun their tires in frustration. Anecdotally, we've heard from many learner-led schools that the students at their schools experienced minor disruptions when pivoting to remote work. A report from Next Generation Learning Challenges (titled "What Made Them So Prepared?") features our school, The Forest School, among others, highlighting how learner-centered, forward-thinking schools with flexible systems were able to meet the challenges of remote learning brought on by the COVID pandemic (Next Generation Learning Challenges, 2022).

We're at an inflection point in education. For the first time, more parents want more things to change about their children's school than stay the same (Populace, 2022). We have seen this in our work. There is an increase in the political will to open up pathways to alternative education. District- and state-level school leaders are actively seeking to boost learner agency in their schools. Traditional schools are struggling with a surge in chronic absenteeism and low motivation among students (Mervosh and Paris, 2024).

Something has to change.

If you've found your way to this book, then you're in the camp of people trying to cultivate self-directed learning in your school. This is hard work, but it's worth it. The bulk of this book will be practical techniques you can use with your team of educators to build a culture of self-directed, independent learners. First, though, we'll explain what we mean when we say self-directed learning and explore common constraints and struggles educators face in this journey.

What is Self-Directed Learning?

There are a lot of terms that get conflated (learner agency, learner-led education, self-determined learning, independent meaningful learning, self-directed education) when talking about learners being in the driver's seat of their own education. We use the term *self-directed learning*. Here's how we define it:

> Self-directed learning is when learners—in the context of an interdependent community of peers, trained educators, and caring adults—choose the process, content, skills, learning pathways, and outcomes of learning, with the guidance, accountability, and support of others, in service of finding a calling that will change their communities and the world.

We see self-directed learning as an umbrella term that captures the heart of the many names given to an education philosophy that centers the learner and their own thoughts, plans, and ideas. A key part of our definition is *community*. When people hear the phrase self-directed learning, they often assume it's a solitary endeavor. However, we always learn via relationships, not in isolation. It was important to us to include community members, including peers, educators, and parents/caregivers, in our understanding of self-directed learning. Another key part of our definition is that the process is *purposeful*. The goal of education should be that young people get meaningful practice at figuring out who they are and what they want to do in the world. Many schools get bogged down in questions of *what* students should learn (content) or *how* students learn (process). For us, the most important questions deal with *why* (purpose). So, even though this book does list practical techniques and is in some ways a "how-to" type of resource, we make a point to define each technique and connect it to a meaningful "why" before we move into the details of how you might implement the technique in your own setting.

Common Constraints

Every learning environment comes with its own set of constraints. Many of you may be interested in boosting learner autonomy in your schools, but you're coming to this book with the mindset that self-directed learning can happen in some schools (with fewer constraints), but not in others (with more constraints). It is our firm belief that learner-led environments can be cultivated in any school and any classroom. It will look different, from context to context. That's the beauty of it! Our goal with this book is not to reproduce our model of self-directed learning in your school. Rather, we want to provoke your thinking and leave you with concrete ways you can move your school community toward greater student agency. Here at the outset, we wanted to name some common constraints and give you some tips on how to work within those constraints to cultivate self-directed learning.

   ♦   *Standards*: National and state standards govern public and charter (and some private) schools. These standards are most felt by educators and students during year-end standardized tests. These tests have become increasingly high stakes and dictate everything from a student's advancement to school funding. The beauty of standards is that they provide clarity to teachers and students about what skills and knowledge count as "mastery" in a given subject area. In our experience, learners in self-directed environments perform better than their peers nationwide on standardized assessments. Here are some creative ways you can incorporate greater autonomy in your classroom while still attending to standards:

◆ Give the standards (in developmentally appropriate language) to students at the beginning of the year. Provide them a "menu" of options they can choose from in how they want to learn those standards. Later in the book, we highlight how a high school sociology and history teacher in Pike County, Georgia uses this approach.

◆ Cultivate the skills of goal setting. Have students set their own goals for how they are going to grow in the knowledge and skills outlined by the standards. Later we tell the story of Jefferson County Open School in Colorado and how they embed goal-setting in everything they do.

◆ Build in a variety of ways for students to display mastery of the standards throughout the year. Test-taking is a subset of skills in itself. Many students that perform well on standardized tests do so because they are good test takers, not necessarily because they deeply know the material. Provide assessments that necessitate actual mastery of the content. These are especially powerful if they are (1) relevant and applicable to a real problem in the world, (2) have public value (they don't die on the teacher's desk), and (3) incorporate feedback from people other than the teacher, preferably with expertise in the relevant field.

◆ Prompt reflection and meta-cognition. Create multiple opportunities for learners to reflect on what they know and what they don't know. A deficit of standardized tests is that they don't allow students to reflect on their mistakes (learners often aren't even aware of what questions they got wrong on a test). Instead, give students plentiful practice at displaying mastery and reflecting on what skills they need to sharpen and knowledge they need to deepen.

◆ *Curriculum*: Another constraint keenly felt by many educators and school leaders is curriculum. Like standards, curriculum is often set by district- and state-level leaders. This often leads educators to feel as if their "hands are tied" in terms of how much experimentation and student-directed projects they can facilitate in the classroom. The upshot of a set curriculum, like standards, is that it provides clarity to all stakeholders about what content will be explored during the school year. Here are a few tips for working within the constraints of curriculum to cultivate learner agency:

  ◆ Give learners the "syllabus" at the beginning of the year. List out the content they are expected to learn (with a reading list and mandatory deliverables). We'll share an example of how the math department at Hall County High School uses this approach to student pacing.

  ◆ Allow learners to adopt their own pacing. Incentivize working through the curriculum early by allowing students to create a "passion project" in a high-interest subject when they finish.

  ◆ Empower learners to do a deep dive into the curriculum. If a student is eager and engaged with the content, provide them ways to further explore (most curriculum will come with extension activities).

  ◆ School leaders and educators should align on the expectations for "coverage" in the curriculum. Many educators assume there is an expectation to cover everything, which is often not the case (and often not possible). This allows the educator more agency in the curriculum development and delivery, and could also open up more opportunities for learner agency as well.

◆ Allow students to choose resources they want to utilize. Distinguish between required texts that all learners are expected to engage with and optional material that students can use or replace with resources they find themselves. Curate relevant and engaging resources that learners can explore further.

◆ Give meaningful choices throughout. Can students choose their deliverables? Can they choose the modalities they are working in? Can they choose their seats or their groups? Can they choose how they are assessed? Even within the constraints of curriculum, learners can make meaningful choices in the way they are engaging with and displaying mastery of the material.

◆ *Grades*: Grading assignments is a major constraint on educators' time and creativity in the classroom. Grades are another one of these edicts seemingly handed down from "on high." Teachers have to grade things. Students have to receive grades. Schools have to track and report grades. It makes sense, then, that so much of traditional schooling revolves around tasks that are easy to grade. Learner-driven projects can be difficult to fit into categories that are easy to grade. So, many educators—even if they see the need to boost student autonomy—will be hesitant to embrace self-directed learning for the sole fact that they're not sure how to grade it and they have a system in place that makes sense to them. So, what can we do? Here are some ways to think about grading in a learner-led classroom:

◆ Grade less. Allow learners to tackle work that's not graded. The fear here is that if we give learners work that's not graded, they won't do it. While not completely unfounded, this fear can be used to reframe a class culture. When students do work just for a grade, they're more focused on "checking boxes" than they are on the material. When the focus shifts from "doing something for a grade" to truly learning the material, learners see the tasks not as busy work, but as an opportunity to grow, practice, and learn. Grading less also goes a long way in easing anxiety among students. Learners are often scared to take risks and make mistakes because they don't want their grade to suffer. By minimizing a "grade-focused" approach to school, learners can be freed up to try things out and learn from their mistakes.

◆ Let learners make the rubric. When giving learners freedom to create their own projects, take the pressure off of educators by giving the learners the responsibility to create their own scoring rubric. The educator can serve the role as coach or facilitator, giving learners feedback on their rubrics and overseeing their creation, but the students themselves are doing the hard work of deciding how they will be assessed. Or, if the rubric is made by the teacher, allow learners to choose how they will demonstrate mastery according to the rubric.

◆ Bring assessment from multiple sources. Instead of the educator always being the evaluator of work, build the skills of learners to assess themselves and their peers. Bring in experts from outside the classroom to weigh in on learners' work. By building in more feedback loops for assessment, teachers can spend less time grading assignments and more time guiding students to learn the material.

- ◆ Use single point rubrics (identifying individual competencies and offering learners feedback on their strengths and weaknesses against that competency) and grade longitudinal growth rather than growth in absolute or comparative ways.
- ◆ *Embracing Failure*: As high-stakes testing has become more and more ingrained in our school cultures, students, teachers, and parents/caregivers have become increasingly risk-averse. Learners don't want to make mistakes. Parents and caregivers don't want their children to experience failure. Teachers see the failure of their students as a reflection of their ability to educate. And so, a culture of avoiding failure has taken root. The stance of this book is that failure is the greatest teacher, especially in a self-directed learning environment. So, what are ways you as a school leader can mitigate against the resistance of learners and their caregivers to *embrace* failure? Here are some ideas:
    - ◆ Model the mindset. How do you as a leader showcase to the community your willingness to adapt, pivot, and learn as you go?
    - ◆ Guide your educators to "self-differentiate." An educator is not ultimately responsible for a student's performance in school. The learner is. The educator's role is to encourage, coach, curate, and facilitate. As a school leader, tie the evaluations of your educators to the fidelity and implementation of your learning design, not to test scores.
    - ◆ Allow learners to experience natural consequences. A by-product of allowing learners to make more *choices* is allowing them to experience the consequences, both positive and negative, from those choices.

We'll address these constraints (and more!) throughout the book as we give specific techniques school leaders and educators can employ in any classroom to move toward greater student agency

Common Struggles

Along with similar design constraints, schools we work with also identify common struggles in moving from traditional, teacher-centered instruction to self-directed learning. We wanted to name these struggles here at the beginning of the book because they're real. They're valid. You will encounter challenges and resistance as you seek to increase learner autonomy. It's hard, messy work. But it's worth it.

Here are some of the struggles you can anticipate in this work:

♦ *Teachers will have a lot to unlearn.* Many classroom teachers have had the traditional way of schooling drilled into their mindsets and habits since they were students themselves. They have deeply rooted assumptions about what the role of a teacher is and how teaching should be done. On top of that, they've had intensive training in the *hows* of teaching, with focus on classroom management, lesson planning, and conducting standardized assessments. The training they received in their teacher-preparation programs has only been reinforced through their in-school experiences, professional development courses, and how they are evaluated by administrators. It's hard to convince an experienced teacher that they should have *less* control in the classroom and give learners *more* responsibility. Many of us educators will have a knee-jerk reaction to that idea and would instead rather rely on doing things the way we've always done them. So, the first struggle to overcome is getting buy-in from your educators. They need to see the *why* behind a concerted move toward student autonomy. Add to that, there will be a "belief gap" in many educators. They won't believe that children are capable of guiding their own learning. As a school leader, you will need to grow their conviction behind this work to make meaningful progress. The best way to do this, we've found, is to have teachers collaborate to design the methods themselves. When we do professional learning for educators, we guide them through the principles of self-directed learning and do some sense-making as a group around the differences of teacher-led and learner-led environments. We then invite educators to bring something they plan on using in class soon (a lesson, assignment, or unit). Then, we ask them to choose two or three of the principles we discussed and revise their work to make it even more learner-centered. They are then given an opportunity to share their ideas with the whole group, which inspires other educators with ideas they can steal shamelessly. As a leader, you can conduct these design sprints often. Bring educators together to brainstorm and tinker. Have them implement their ideas. Then, invite them back together to discuss how it went. As you do this, teachers will identify the barriers that they face in moving their classrooms toward greater student agency. You, as a leader, can identify which barriers you can remove or minimize, and which are beyond your control. For those teachers struggling to believe that kids really are capable, you can invite them to test their hypothesis. Have them run experiments in learner agency and see what happens. Build a culture of sharing and learning so that teacher teams can hear what other educators are successfully doing in their classrooms (and consider inviting them to visit and observe other schools that are cultivating self-directed learners). A great way to get buy-in from your educators is to make sure their fingerprints are all over the learning design. Beyond teacher-designed methods, the practical techniques in this book will help equip *you* to further empower *them* to shift toward learner-centered education.

◆ *Parents and caregivers may initially be confused or skeptical.*
Adults generally base their expectations of schooling on

their own educational experiences. We have our own assumptions about what school is and how it should be done. Most parents and caregivers will expect their children to have experiences similar to their own, which was most likely teacher-centered direct instruction. Parents expect their kids will go to school and *be taught* what they need to know. When you start talking about self-directed learning and how children really need to grow in their ability to learn how to learn, parents and caregivers will get suspicious. We've had one ask us, "If they're teaching themselves, why am I sending them to school?" That's a valid question. As a school leader, you'll also have to build the conviction of your parents and caregivers around *why* your school is focusing on boosting learner agency. It's not a hard sell to make. It's easy to point to the ways that our school system is falling short in cultivating independent learners. Many parents and caregivers saw this first-hand during the pandemic, when schooling moved remote and they saw how dependent their children were on having a teacher tell them what to do and when to do it. There are a lot of valid reasons (backed by data and anecdotal evidence) to move toward learner-led education. You (as a school leader) have to be intentional about making the case to your community and getting the parents and caregivers involved from the beginning. We'll provide techniques throughout the book for you to utilize (like Parent Coffees, Onboarding, Curated Resources, and Conferences), but it's important to note that parents and caregivers will need to be guided on their own learning journey.

◆ *Students themselves might resist change.* Let's face it, it's easier to have someone tell you how to do something. It's easier to have someone answer all your questions. It's easier to have someone explain everything to you. It's easier to feel like you're not solely responsible for when and how (or even if) you do your work. Kids know this. When you begin to shift the responsibility of learning toward the learners, they'll be hesitant to take it on. Not all of them. Some of your students have been waiting for this moment and will take as much autonomy as you'll hand them. Many, though, will struggle. It will be common for them to see themselves as victims and shift blame. There's a temptation here to step in—as school leaders, educators, and caregivers—and keep the learners from experiencing this frustration. *Don't*. It's crucial that students experience this shift in responsibility, as uncomfortable as it is. Once they realize that their learning is really on them, in a meaningful way, and that no one is going to step in and do the work for them, they're ready to take the first baby steps toward greater agency. They quickly learn how to walk, then run. We hinder their growth when we try to intervene too much in this early stage. Anecdotally (this isn't scientific data), we tell families that it will take one month for every year a child has received direct instruction before they move out of this stage of frustration. So, a student that has been in a teacher-centered environment for eight, nine, or ten years may take a full school year before they start really shouldering responsibility for their own learning (we've seen it happen multiple times). Give them as much time as possible—with plenty of resources and encouragement along the way. Again, given the constraints we highlighted earlier, it may not seem like you have time to give. Our encouragement: don't rush the process. Provide learners with meaningful choice (which includes the choice not to do something) and allow them to experience the consequences of those choices. Creating a learner-led environment is playing a long game. You're cultivating skills, habits, and mindsets in young people that may not take hold for months or years. Don't give up.

◆ *It's messy*. As one school leader told us, "The work is beautiful, but it ain't always pretty." As leaders and educators, we are often trying to control or manage a school setting and mitigate against learning that could appear chaotic. Giving learners more autonomy means there may invariably be more distractions (students talking, moving around the classroom, etc.). Part of developing strong self-regulation skills in students is allowing for this messiness to unfold *while* they are receiving coaching and support from educators. Over time, learners will develop their own strategies (like wearing noise-canceling headphones) and learn where and how they learn best (like choosing not to sit beside their friends while they need to focus on work). Students will also develop skills in conflict resolution as they navigate how to get work done alongside their peers. They'll learn how to negotiate in ways similar to how adults interact with coworkers. The learning that happens—even in the midst of messiness—provides ample practice for young people on learning how to live and work with others.

Pioneers in Public Spaces

There has been an explosion of self-directed learning models in the past two decades. The majority of these are small, independent microschools. Many of these schools are part of rapidly expanding networks (like Acton Academy and Prenda). The pace at which these schools and networks have been able to scale highlights the demand that exists for learner-led environments. A recent study by Mosaic revealed that 74% of parents surveyed across the U.S. were interested in learning more about self-directed schools (Veneski and Breen, 2023). Some proponents of self-directed learning see this rapidly expanding network of small schools as the answer to an outdated public education system that has increasingly stripped agency from teachers and learners alike in the move toward standardization. Others, though, argue that the growth of these private spaces weakens investment in public education. Can self-directed learning be embraced without forsaking a commitment to public education?

Our answer is an emphatic yes!

There are dozens of school districts and charter networks working to increase student agency. We'll highlight many of them throughout the book, but here are a few pioneers of self-directed learning in public spaces:

◆ **Northern Cass Schools, North Dakota**: Northern Cass began their shift to self-directed learning in 2017. The school district was successful by most metrics (test scores and GPAs), but felt like they weren't serving kids enough in terms of cultivating independence. We highlight two of their techniques in this book. One, called Studios, is a self-directed learning pathway for high school students. Learners can choose to take courses traditionally, or they can opt into a customized Studio experience to replace the course. In Studios, they meet with a learning coach to design a high-interest project. Then, they align the standards of whatever course they are replacing (e.g., World History) to the project design. Students create their own milestones and schedule for deliverables and present final products at the end of their Studio. The second technique we highlight is a peer-mentorship program called Luminaries. Luminaries are juniors and seniors who have received intensive training in giving high-quality peer feedback. Luminaries schedule time to be in the library, where other students can sign up for one-on-one mentorship and feedback sessions.

◆ **Pike County Schools, Georgia**: Under the leadership of superintendent Mike Duncan, Pike County made some drastic shifts toward self-directed learning. The district put "self-directed learning" as one of three pillars in the Pike Instructional Framework. Mike taught an elective course called "How to Change the World." The course was designed to be an open-inquiry, self-directed, design-thinking challenge. Learners spent many weeks learning about design thinking, completing fun, fast design challenges, practicing goal setting, feedback, and reflection. The culminating event was a Ted Talk-style event where students discussed the project, the process, and their learning. Mike then invited interested teachers to join optional professional development workshops to cultivate self-directed learning in their classrooms. Those teachers are still carrying the torch of learner-centered education in their classes. We highlight many of their in-class strategies throughout the book.

◆ **Logan County Schools, Kentucky**: Logan County built self-directed learning into their learning model. Using the design principles below, Logan County created a Profile of Success (which we call a Profile of a Graduate later in the book) that highlights self-directed skills. To graduate, students must pass a Defense of Learning, a learner-led assessment where learners showcase their mastery of all the competencies in the Profile of Success. We highlight their approach later in the book when we discuss the assessment technique of Practicals. Here are the principles that animate their learning design:

  ◆ *Whole Child*: ensuring each child, in each school, in each community is healthy, safe, engaged, supported, and challenged.

  ◆ *Learner Agency*: recognizes the unique interests and passions of every learner and makes them the primary agents of their learning.

  ◆ *Competency-Based*: instruction, assessment, grading, and academic reporting are based on students demonstrating that they have learned the knowledge and skills they are expected to learn as they progress through their education.

- *Learner Centered Community*: development of skills, combined with opportunities, to engage in meaningful collaboration to learn, innovate, and solve meaningful challenges that matter to individuals and the greater community.
- *Relevant and Authentic*: students explore, discuss, and meaningfully construct concepts and relationships in contexts that involve real-world problems and projects that are relevant to the learner.
- *Personalized*: Aims to customize learning for each student's strengths, needs, skills, and interests.

◆ **Mineola Public Schools, New York**: Mineola Public Schools (under the leadership of superintendent Michael Nagler) launched a self-directed high school as a pilot, not only for the district, but as a dramatic example for the country to follow. The school, called Synergy, is designed to give students choice over their work and combines career exploration, hands-on projects, and mental health supports to cultivate a relevant and engaging learning environment. Instead of siloed class periods, learners meet together in a large space with flexible seating options (couches and drafting tables). They start their day with a one-on-one meeting with a mentor teacher and set their goals around what they will be working on and for how long. These goals are recorded and presented on a large screen in the space for clarity, alignment, and accountability. Subject area teachers upload all lessons and materials to an online platform and are available to field questions or support learners if needed. At the end of the day, learners meet with their mentor teachers for a "checkout," where they debrief and reflect on their progress and roadblocks. If learners are consistently struggling to independently meet their goals, teachers step in and assign direct instruction or mandatory small-group work. Synergy is not a 'one-size-fits-all' environment, but a school dedicated to personalized learning for each and every student.

◆ **Jefferson County Open School, Colorado**: The Open School has been around since the 1970s. The mission statement of the school reads: "The Open School provides a dynamic environment that fosters the development of the unique potential in each individual by nurturing and challenging the whole person. There is an emphasis on self-direction, learning through experience, shared responsibility, and the development of life long-skills" (Jefferson County Open School, 2024). The school is built on the concept of personalized learning. Each student works with an advisor to create a Mutually Agreed-upon Plan (MAP). The MAP may involve a mix of traditionally styled courses that focus heavily on lectures, collaborative laboratories and workshops, internships and apprenticeships outside of school, and other learning activities. The MAP is customized to each student and provides maximum flexibility for learners and their families to *choose* their own outcomes and pathways.

History also illuminates potential pathways forward in how private and public schools can learn from each other. A famous example is John Dewey's laboratory school at the University of Chicago (Mayhew and Edwards, 1936). Dewey was a proponent of public education, though critical of the pedagogies entrenched in teacher education programs and replicated in schoolhouses. The laboratory school was just that—a place to experiment with pedagogical approaches and curriculum design that placed the learner at the center of the learning project. The goal for Dewey was not to replace public education with a network of private or university-based elementary schools. Rather, Dewey wanted to use the laboratory school as a testing ground whose influence would radiate outward, into other universities, teacher's colleges, and school districts. The laboratory school—though intentionally designed to be different than Industrial Age schools—was created to save public education, not destroy it.

Likewise, the proliferation of self-directed spaces in recent years provides ample opportunities for researchers, policymakers, and educators to see learner-led education in action. For this reason, we co-founded the Institute for Self-Directed Learning to be housed within The Forest School, our lab school. The goal of the Institute is to take all that is being learned through experimentation with learner-led pedagogies in a PreK-12 setting and share this information widely with public school partners. Part of the work is teacher-specific (how can teachers in public schools make micro-moves toward self-directed learning in their own classrooms?), part of the work is district-level, partnering with school leaders to cultivate more learner-led public schools (sometimes as school-within-school options), and part of the work is at the policy level, working to create the sort of research that might convince policymakers someday that public education really is worth the investment and that self-directed pedagogies have much to say to current problems in the design and functioning of the nation's public education system.

A Brief Outline

We have divided the techniques in this book across ten chapters. The goal was to create meaningful categories so that you can easily search out the strategies most relevant to you. So, we've grouped techniques into chapters around themes like goal setting, pacing, and assessment. One way to read this text is to jump around to the chapters most applicable to your current scenario and learning goals. However, we've also designed this book to build on itself. The chapters are arranged in a logical order. We start with cultivating relationships, which anyone who has been in schools for any length of time will say are crucial to doing this work well. We end on assessment and environmental factors. To familiarize you to the way we'll be grouping the techniques, let us briefly orient you to the chapter breakdown.

- ◆ *Forming and Weaving Networks of Relationships*: All educators know the importance of cultivating strong relationships with students. In a self-directed learning environment, educators not only form strong bonds with students, but also equip young people with the skills and mindsets to build and strengthen their own social networks. In this chapter, we outline techniques for empowering learners to form and weave valuable networks of relationships.
- ◆ *Focusing on the Whole Child*: Education is not merely about academic growth. It's about forming self-determined young people of character who are well-equipped to lead a flourishing life. This chapter highlights techniques on cultivating holistic growth in your school community.
- ◆ *Promoting Student and Educator Choice*: The heart of self-directed learning is the ability for young people to make meaningful choices about their own education. In this chapter, we discuss techniques for providing meaningful choice for students and teachers.
- ◆ *Facilitating Daily Student Goal Setting*: Self-directed learners are well-equipped to set their own learning goals. We provide techniques for cultivating the skills of students to identify their long-term learning goals and set meaningful, measurable short-term goals to get there. This chapter provides a menu of techniques for building the skills of goal-setting.
- ◆ *Organizing for Student Self-Pacing*: A key piece of self-directed learning is the ability for young people to have choice in the pace of their work. Some students will want to work faster than they currently can in their classroom. Some will want to take longer. This chapter provides techniques and creative ways for educators to consider pacing, even within the constraints of traditional education.

◆ *Empowering Students' Rule Making*: Most students spend their days following rules they had no say in making. A way to build a positive classroom culture is to give students real, meaningful choice in the rule-making process. This chapter highlights techniques for guiding your young people to create and enforce their own rules.

◆ *Nurturing Exploration*: Young people are curious. They love to explore, inquire, and make meaning of the world. Unfortunately, the way we go about education often strips this natural curiosity from children. In this chapter, we provide techniques for attending to the innate inquisitiveness of students and making space for their own exploration.

◆ *Embracing Productive Struggle*: Often, we (as parents, caregivers, and educators) try to shield young people from experiencing failure. Making mistakes, though—and learning from natural consequences—provide the greatest learning experiences a person can have. In this chapter, we discuss techniques for how school leaders and educators can design for and provide right-sized challenges that allow students to experience productive struggle.

◆ *Facilitating Learner-Led Assessment*: The current state of education is assessment-driven. The weight of performing well on standardized tests is felt by school leaders, teachers, students, and parents/caregivers. In this chapter, we offer techniques on low-stakes/high-impact assessments that include learner self-assessments, peer reviews, and expert evaluations.

◆ *Designing the Environment*: The learning environment itself (room layout, furniture, decor, etc.) was a primary focus of education reformers like Maria Montessori and John Dewey. In this chapter, we give techniques for designing a learner-centered classroom, offering simple (yet helpful) tips on how attending to your learning environment can in and of itself promote self-directed learning.

Again, in each chapter we'll clarify what component of your school model needs to change to implement each strategy, as well as the biggest ripple effects across your system.

Words of Wisdom

We reached out to educators utilizing self-directed learning in their classroom. When asked about the one takeaway they would share with other educators, this is what they said:

> …there have been fewer discipline issues with students because when students are in the driver's seat and not just hanging out in the backseat waiting for you to drive them to an unknown destination, they feel like they are taking an active role in their education!
>
> High school history teacher

> Here…we were allowed and encouraged to take risks. In previous systems, I had to worry if the lesson became messy and didn't work out the way I planned. [In this district], I have grown comfortable in the mess. Sometimes things don't go to plan, but more often than not, my students reach a deeper understanding and use problem solving to create higher-level products. One major change in my way of teaching is that I no longer have to know everything. I often create [projects] in which there isn't one answer, and I don't know the answers. I try to leave more options open for my students to discover their own path.
>
> High school math teacher

> I think about one student I had that didn't like school. It was obvious. I had her in first grade and she moved up to second grade with me. But this year, after trying self-directed learning, [she] came up to me and said 'Can we do this again? It was fun learning with my friends.' The

more I released responsibility to the students, the more excited she became about school.

Elementary school teacher

There are many more quotes we could include, and you will encounter more stories and testimonials as you read. A theme, though, as we have talked with educators about shifting towards self-directed learning is that *their job becomes richer and more enjoyable*. They see a significant decrease in problematic behaviors. They see a boost in engagement and motivation. They dispel the myth that they have to be the knowledge experts with all the answers. As they hand off tasks to learners, they find they have more time to engage with the fun work of education like designing challenges, coaching and guiding learners to explore their curiosities, and cultivating deeper relationships through check-ins and conversations.

A Call to Action

How you use this text is up to you. We hope that it provokes you to think deeply about how you are empowering the young people in your school to live choice-filled lives. The techniques listed here are starting points. We came to them through our own experience of running a learner-led microschool as well as meeting and working with school leaders (public, private, and charter) from around the world who are seeking to cultivate greater learner agency in their schools.

This book is not just a collection of strategies but a call to action. It invites you to rethink how education is delivered and to experiment with and refine these approaches in your school setting. Our ultimate goal is to demonstrate ways you can prepare students to be self-directed learners who are equipped to navigate a rapidly changing world. We believe that this transformation in education is essential for developing future generations who are not only knowledgeable but also adaptable and resilient.

References

Hammond, Z. (2014). *Culturally Responsive Teaching and the Brain: Promoting Authentic Engagement and Rigor Among Culturally and Linguistically Diverse Students*. Corwin Press.

Jefferson County Open School (2024). https://jcos.jeffcopublicschools.org

Lemov, D. (2021). *Teach Like a Champion 3.0: 63 Techniques that Put Students on the Path to College*. Jossey-Bass.

Mayhew, K., & Edwards, A. (1936). *The Dewey School: The laboratory School of the University of Chicago, 1896–1903*. D. Appleton-Century Company.

Mervosh, S., & Paris, F. (2024, March 29). Why school absences have 'Exploded' almost everywhere. *The New York Times*. https://www.nytimes.com/interactive/2024/03/29/us/chronic-absences.html

Moss Brown, M. and Berger, A. (2014). *How to Innovate: The Essential Guide for Fearless School Leaders*. Teachers College Press.

Next Generation Learning Challenges. (2022). "What Made Them So Prepared? Why these schools and districts could take on COVID effectively—and what you can learn from them." https://www.nextgenlearning.org/prepared-project

Populace Inc. (2022). *Populace Insights: Purpose of Education Index*. https://static1.squarespace.com/static/59153bc0e6f2e109b2a85cbc/t/63e96b44a0e46d79a10ecf26/1676241761790/Purpose+of+Education+Index.pdf

Stixrud, W. and Johnson, N. (2018). *The Self-Driven Child: The Science and Sense of Giving Your Kids More Control Over Their Lives*. Viking.

Veneski, W. and Breen, A. (2023). "Self-Directed Education (SDE) National Survey Executive Summary" *Mosaic*. https://assets.ctfassets.net/teg0415w6bj9/6z0OyuqEFEWKYNR70NFtMI/fe45b781e503094f1402258b1a73101d/220725._Mosaic__Research_Branded_Executive_Summary.pdf

2

Forming and Weaving Networks of Relationships

A common misconception of self-directed learning is that it is something that you do alone, on your own, without input, feedback, or collaboration with others. Learning is by nature relational. Humans learn from other humans. As babies and young people, we observe and mimic. As we get older, we inquire and converse. We explore resources created by others—books, videos, and exemplars. We learn in community, from our parents, mentors, peers, and experts we meet along the way.

As a school leader, perhaps your greatest role is to build and maintain relationships with parents, staff, and learners. In this chapter, we'll highlight the techniques you can use across those stakeholder groups. First, though, we'll lay out some brief concepts, arguments, and anecdotes to highlight the importance of relationships for learning.

DOI: 10.4324/9781003489894-2

A Story

When co-author Tyler was 12 years old, his parents told him if he wanted a car, he would have to pay for it himself. That's how Tyler became an entrepreneur. He started a business cutting grass, named it Executive Lawn Care, and began pushing his mower. Sure enough, by the time he was 16 he made $5,500 and purchased his very first car—a 1989 black Chevrolet Blazer. For a while Tyler reflected on that story with pride: "Look how hard I worked. I sacrificed a lot. Thanks to my hard work and determination I was able to make the money and buy this car for myself." The older he got, though, the more he reflected. The more families he got to know, the more Tyler began to realize it wasn't just his efforts that made his business venture a success. First, it was his parents' mower—they lent it to him. Second, cutting grass wasn't Tyler's idea to begin with. A friend gave it to him. It was Tyler's grandfather who taught him how to open a bank account and save money over time. It was each of his neighbors who were willing to trust a middle schooler instead of hiring a professional landscaping company. It was a network of relationships that made the whole thing possible.

We want young people to shoulder responsibility. We want them to grow in their abilities to go out and direct their own lives. This sense of "agency" and "responsibility" is cultivated first and foremost through a deep network of supporting relationships.

The Heart of Self-Directed Learning

At the heart of self-directed learning is the idea that students take responsibility for their own education. They set their own goals, choose their own learning activities, and monitor their own progress. They work at their own pace with tools and strategies they prefer. Self-directed learners are highly independent, but self-directed learning is not independent study. No child is an island. Supportive relationships are the avenue through which self-directed learners thrive.

Since 1938, Harvard has been conducting "The Harvard Study of Adult Development." Its purpose is to identify the factors that lead to a flourishing life. For 85 years they've been observing the lives of a group of boys from low-income families in Boston, and a group of Harvard male undergraduates. They've been documenting the lives of these men as they've grown from early boyhood into late life. Participants offer regular information about their relationships and personal wellbeing. They share medical records and financial gains and losses. They report professional success and failure, crises and celebration, and other various details to help researchers understand what causes human flourishing. The study reveals a great number of things, but among their discoveries one speaks the loudest: people who cultivate meaningful relationships live longer, happier lives. The lead researchers, Robert Waldinger and Marc Shulz, summed up the project this way: "if we had to take all eighty-four years of the Harvard Study and boil it down to a single principle for living, one life investment that is supported by similar findings across a wide variety of other studies, it would be this: Good relationships keep us healthier and happier. Period" (2023).

What is Social Capital?

Practical help emerges from caring relationships. We know in today's world that success is not just about what you know, it is also about who you know. A substantial portion of job opportunities are accessed through personal networks and connections. According to research (Fisher, 2020), over 80% of jobs are filled through networking and around 70% of jobs are never posted publicly. Helping learners foster community expands real-world experiences and opportunities.

This is what is known as "Social Capital," the help that emerges from trusting, caring relationships. Social capital provides people with access to information, knowledge, skills, and expertise. It cultivates a sense of belonging and support. Within the context of education, social capital has been shown to be a critical factor for success, particularly in self-directed learning environments.

When learners have strong social capital, they are more likely to have access to a diverse range of resources, including peers, mentors, experts, and other professionals who can offer guidance and support. This access can help learners overcome obstacles. This can be especially valuable for learners who do not have access to these resources otherwise. With a strong network of relationships, learners can develop the ability to work in teams, communicate, and problem-solve effectively—all essential skills for life in the real world.

When learners have strong social capital, they feel a sense of community and belonging, which motivates them to engage more deeply with their learning. This sense of belonging helps learners build confidence and self-efficacy. When learners have a strong network of relationships, they can connect with individuals who work in their desired fields, attend conferences and events, and participate in extracurricular activities, all of which can broaden their perspectives and expose them to new ideas and experiences. Self-directed learning prioritizes building and fostering social capital among learners to improve their outcomes and prepare them for success in the future.

Relationship-building is not just a fundamental value of education, but a fundamental value of life. It is through our connections with others that we find meaning, purpose, and fulfillment, and it is through these relationships that we can make a positive impact on the world around us. As school leaders, we recognize the importance of relationship-building in our work as a fundamental value of our practice. We strive to create learning environments built on trust, mutual respect, and understanding, and we work to develop meaningful connections with our communities.

By cultivating relationships with others, learners can rely on a network of support as they take risks and learn to make their own decisions. In knowing and being known by others, they gain access to a wealth of knowledge, experience, resources, and opportunities. They ask questions, receive feedback on their work, and seek guidance for how to improve and grow. Through positive relationships, self-led learners hone the skills of collaboration and find courage to achieve their goals.

What is a Flourishing Network?

As the saying goes, "it takes a village." Children grow into maturity through a series of caring relationships. Family, like parents, grandparents, aunts and uncles, siblings, and cousins. Peer relationships. Coaches and mentors. Educators. Siblings. Pastors, imams, and rabbis. Surrounding each child is a web of caring adults. Often, the greatest indicator of how successful that child's future will be is the strength and breadth of that network.

School leaders have a critical role to play in helping learners cultivate these relationships. They're in a position better than most to provide opportunities for students to interact with individuals from backgrounds and perspectives they may not be able to otherwise access on their own. Every activity, whether it be a classroom discussion, group project, or even a test, provides an opportunity to help students build and nurture their relationships and networks. Group projects can help students develop collaboration skills and build relationships with their peers. Classroom discussions can encourage students to listen to and understand different perspectives. Tests are opportunities for students to support each other and participate in study groups.

Sometimes we educators often focus on the technical aspects of teaching: developing lesson plans, implementing strategies, and assessing learning outcomes. While these elements are critical to the learning process, the fundamental value that underpins all of these activities is relationship-building. Relationships are the foundation of all learning and the secret sauce to flourishing. In this chapter, we'll share practical techniques for helping learners expand and enrich their social capital.

The Techniques

Here are our techniques leaders can use to help form and weave supportive relationships for their educators, students, and their families:

Relationship-Centered, Vision-Aligned Onboarding

System Element: Vision/School Concept

Biggest Ripple Effect: Assessment (measuring the quality and quantity of children's relationships).

What it is and Why:

As a school leader, you're familiar with onboarding new students and team members. In a learner-centered environment, though, you're not just onboarding people to an organization, you're building conviction and buy-in for a model of education that will most likely be new to them. As such, you will likely need to create new (and continually re-assess and re-create) protocols for onboarding staff, parents/caregivers, and learners.

New team members, parents/caregivers, and learners will each come with their own expectations about school. It is the role of the school leader to effectively communicate the vision, highlight potential barriers, and provide right-sized resources to onboard stakeholders. We encourage you to have three streams of onboarding: one for parents/caregivers, one for staff, and one for learners. We also encourage you to make each process "self-directed," so that everyone experiences what you're trying to achieve at the school.

How to do it:

The leader's role is to:
1. Cast a clear vision.
    1. Why does the school exist? What is its mission? What is the "Portrait of a Graduate" the school aspires to?
    2. Tap into the hopes that parents and caregivers have for their children. Ask the community what traits they value the most to cultivate in their children. Create connections between their aspirations for their children and the vision of your school.
2. Create a comprehensive process for team members, parents/caregivers, and learners.
    1. Curate resources (packets, links, videos) that explain the systems and processes of the school.
    2. Make the resources "right-sized." It can be easy to overwhelm new community members with too much material, delivered too soon.
    3. Provide avenues for discussion so that new community members can "sense make" together and ask questions.
    4. Provide feedback loops to capture lingering questions, gaps in the materials, or suggestions for how to revise the onboarding process.

5. Pair new families with veteran families. See your school community as a resource and create a light-lift process for existing families to mentor newly admitted ones.

3. Have a "finish line." What does it look like for a new educator to fully embody the mission and ethos of the school? What about a new learner? Create a "rite of passage" that recognizes community members who cross this threshold.

The educator's role is to:

1. Clearly define expectations, norms, and deliverables to new learners.
    1. For new learners, what does it look like to be successful? How will they know if they are on track? How will they be evaluated?
    2. What are the rules and norms? What is standard versus what is customizable? Where do learners have freedom?
    3. Define terms and jargon. Translate the culture of the classroom into easy-to-understand words.
2. Provide a graduated process for learners to complete some form of onboarding.
    1. Do they need to read materials before stepping foot into the classroom? Do they need to create something to share with peers beforehand? Is there a process for becoming familiar with the class expectations *before* they dive into standard learning experiences?
    2. How are new learners receiving feedback from peers and educators?
    3. What systems/protocols are in place for new learners to ask questions/seek clarification from peers and educators?

3. Create a "finish line" and celebrate new learners that cross it!
    1. What does it mean for a learner to become a full member of the community? Is there a "public" way for them to take that step? At The Forest School, we have a moment where every learner signs their name to the Rules and Promises they created as a community. What sort of "crossing the threshold" ritual will you have in place?

Dream Teams

System Element: Community Practices and School Culture

Biggest Ripple Effect: Schedules and Routines (to make time for this), Roles (for teachers and leaders to crowdsource mentoring relationships), and Facilities (making space for it).

What it is and why:
Many schools have found success in utilizing Dream Teams to support learners (a practice that emerged from Transcend's early work with Achievement First Greenefield in New Haven, Connecticut). The Dream Team is a support system of trusted, knowledgeable adults who care about the learner and want them to succeed. At the beginning of each school year, learners select and nominate family members, friends, and mentors to be a part of their Dream Team. The Dream Team carries learners through their learning journey by providing counsel, resources, and opportunities, encouraging their pursuits, and holding them accountable to their goals. Dream Teams meet on a semi-regular basis to discuss what the learner's goals are, the progress they've made, and changes they want to make. Learners take the lead by making the agenda and facilitating the meetings. Dream Team members respond and provide support, accountability, and inspiration.

We encourage learners to assemble their Dream Teams three times a year: a meeting to kick off the start of the year, a midway check in, and an end of the year update. In these learner-led meetings, the learner sets the agenda. During the first meeting, learners set the tone and expectations for the group, and present their goals for the year. The Dream Team is able to speak into those goals, and let the learner know how they can and cannot help. During their mid-year check in, learners reassemble the Dream Team to provide an update: "This is what I said I wanted to do, and here's where I am." The Dream Team is able to again speak into those goals, lending their bias and expertise. During the end of year review, learners share how their school year went, what they're excited about, what they are bummed about, the challenges they faced, what they overcame, and what they learned.

How to do it:

The role of the educator is to
1. Introduce Dream Teams to learners at the start of the year, and prompt them to consider their nominations.
2. Help learners craft language and send the invitation for their Dream Team to assemble.
3. Guide learners to plan their meeting agendas.
4. Encourage learners to schedule a meeting at the start of the year to gather with their Dream Teams and share their goals.
5. Encourage learners to schedule mid-year and end-of-year follow-up meetings to share their progress and seek counsel from a trusted network.

The role of the learner is to
1. Nominate members of their Dream Team
2. Invite the Dream Team to assemble three times a year

3. Plan and lead the agenda for each of these meetings
4. Connect with the Dream Team throughout the year whenever support, counsel, or help with an opportunity is needed.

What you need:

♦ Time at the start of the year to introduce Dream Teams and guide learners to nominate and assemble their members.

♦ Time to help learners determine how they will present their goals, needs, and progress.

♦ Resources: Achievement First Greenfield pioneered Dream Teams (Greenfield Dream Teams – The Exchange, 2023). You can learn more by visiting their resources on Transcend's Innovative Models Exchange (https:// exchange.transcendeducation.org/models/greenfield-dream-teams/)

The gist:

Dream Teams are one of the most powerful mechanisms learners have for building the muscles of self-direction and ownership, and for realizing it's not just them on their own—they need a community that supports and celebrates them. Dream Teams facilitate a way for learners to have support outside of the school as well as within. It's a way for them to build their social capital over time, developing relationships with people who can give them access to resources and networks they might not have otherwise had.

Check-Ins

System Element: Community Practices and School Culture

Biggest Ripple Effect: Pedagogy (teachers as guides), Schedules and Routines (to make time for this), Roles (for educators to provide one-on-one guidance and coaching; staff have to be deployed in creative ways to make this happen), and Facilities (making space for it).

What it is and why:
The relationship between a learner and their educator is foundational. One way to cultivate this relationship is through regular one-on-one "check-ins." The cadence of this will depend on your class size and schedule. We encourage you to find a rhythm that works and be consistent. In these learner-led check-ins, students discuss their goals and deadlines, pose questions, identify the obstacles in their way, strategize solutions, and celebrate wins. Educators honor students' own goals, ask questions, offer feedback, provoke deeper critical thinking, and help learners connect with supportive resources. These are great opportunities for educators to ask learners about their Dream Teams and how they are utilizing the support of the caring adults in their lives. These meetings help keep learners on track and offer educators a chance to understand each learner's progress and areas of need. Check-ins are one of the main ways educators develop positive relationships with self-determined learners. These frequent, one-on-one meetings help students know they are not alone.

How to do it:

The educator's role is to:
1. Get a snapshot of where learners are on their goals.
    1. Ask each learner what happened since the last meeting. What did you do? What went well? What didn't? How did you manage your challenges? How did you celebrate your wins?
2. Help learners identify their needs.
    1. Ask each learner what they think is needed next. Are you missing any important resources? Do you need

to connect with anyone? Do you need to strengthen a weak spot? Do you need to plan or manage your progress differently?

3. Help learners discover what they can do differently.

    1. Ask questions to get each learner to reflect on how they might adjust their approach in the week(s) ahead. What has worked so far and can you reproduce that result? What didn't work and why? What's something different you can try instead? Offer positive feedback and prompt them to consider possibilities they may not perceive.

4. Provide accountability.

    1. Ask how they intend to accomplish their upcoming goals. What are your goals next week? Are they realistic? What's your plan for accomplishing them? How will you know if you're successful? What can you do if you come off track?

The learner's role is to:

1. Come to the check-in prepared.

2. Review what happened since the last check-in.

    1. Encourage your learners to share any academic, social, and/or personal events that felt meaningful to them. Ask open-ended questions that prompt the learner to self-reflect and process their efforts and outcomes.

3. Discuss challenges and wins.

    1. Listen without judgment as learners share their victories and roadblocks. Celebrate their wins together, and empathize with their struggles. Instead of offering advice, Guides should ask questions to prompt learners to investigate what led to each instance of success or error.

4. Strategize next steps.

    1. Help learners build their own strategies and solve their own problems by guiding them to think through

possibilities. Instead of telling them what to do, ask learners to consider what has worked before, what else they'd like to try, and what kind of resources they'll need in order to be successful.

5. Set goals and create a schedule.

  1. Encourage learners to set goals that are both challenging and realistic. As learners set goals, focus on "what" and "why" questions. What do you want to accomplish, and why? As learners create a schedule, focus on helping them see and organize their priorities, determine important milestones, and be realistic in setting timelines for themselves.

What educators need to successfully implement check-ins:

♦ Time in the schedule! This is going to be the biggest barrier to scaling check-ins, as schedules for educators and learners are already full. As a school leader, how can you free up your educators to have frequent check-ins with learners? They can range in length (we recommend 10 to 30 minutes) and frequency (we recommend at least monthly). For example, a middle school teacher with six classes per day and 30 students per class can structure monthly check-ins by either meeting with small groups of five students daily in each class, rotating daily check-ins with five students from a different class each day, or checking in with five individual students per class each week. The important thing is that they are learner-led, related to the learner's own goals, and give the educator a snapshot into the inner lives of their learners.

♦ A template of questions to ask, what notes to take, progress to measure, and tips for following up.

The Gist:

If we are intentional about building relationships with learners in little moments throughout the year, they are more ready to open up when it counts. When learners feel supported in their self-directed endeavors, they feel safe to take on bigger challenges (like graduating early) and face roadblocks (like tricky social dynamics). Students can accomplish more than we believe when they are surrounded by a network of consistent, supportive relationships. Check-ins provide a built-in, regular time for educators to sew into the lives of their learners.

Social Capital Tracker

System Element: Assessment

Biggest Ripple Effect: Tech and Tech Infrastructure (to keep track of relationship networks) and Roles (seeing and including people outside of school as key stakeholders).

What it is and why:
Healthy social capital can be divided into three main types of relationships: bridges, bonds, and links. Each of these types of relationships are vital to the development of a strong social network. The idea of "bridges, bonds, and links" comes from the work of sociologist Nan Lin, who developed the concept of social capital in the 1980s (Lin, 2002). Lin argued that social capital is a valuable resource that individuals can use to achieve their goals and aspirations.

Bridging social capital refers to connections between people who have meaningfully different backgrounds. These relationships provide access to new information, resources, and opportunities that might not be available through one's immediate social networks. Bridging social capital is important for creating social and economic opportunities, particularly for individuals who are members of disadvantaged or marginalized groups.

Bonding social capital, on the other hand, refers to connections between people who share similar identities or characteristics, such as race, ethnicity, religion, or socioeconomic status. These relationships provide emotional support, a sense of belonging, and a shared understanding of one another's experiences. Bonding social capital builds trust and solidarity within communities and often becomes a reliable source of social and emotional support.

Linking social capital refers to connections between people at different levels of power or status, such as those between individuals and institutions or those between individuals and people in positions of authority. These relationships provide access to resources and opportunities that might not be available through one's immediate social networks. Linking social capital helps individuals access resources that can open doors and unlock opportunities along their path. As learners are building their Dream Teams, it's important for them to have each type of social capital represented.

As a way to organize, visualize, and monitor a learner's social capital, at The Forest School we've developed a simple tool called a Social Capital Tracker. As the name implies, a Social Capital Tracker is about keeping track of each learner's social capital growth. Through a Social Capital Tracker, educators help learners monitor their own progress and assess the strength of the relationships they have with folks who are like them (bonds), folks who are different from them (bridges), and with folks who are in power (links). Even elementary age learners can and should track their social capital.

How to do it:
Each learner has their own Social Capital Tracker. It's a simple sheet of paper or online document where learners can list the relationships they have in each of the three categories. Over time, learners are able to revise and update their document as they get to know more people. This technique helps learners become aware of the gaps in their social network and do something intentional about it.

My Social Network

Your social capital is the network of relationships that you have that serve as a resource and support system for you as you move along your Hero's Journey. For the categories below, think about people you would go to if you needed help or support. These should be deep friendships and relationships, not just acquaintances. In each column, please put the person's name and some form of contact information (email or phone number).

People I am closely connected to who are like me:	People I am closely connected to who are different than me:	People I am closely connected to who are in positions of power:
1.	1.	1.
2.	2.	2.
3.	3.	3.
4.	4.	4.

FIGURE 2.1 Social Capital Tracker. Tool created by The Forest School.

The role of the educator is to

1. Provide materials (pen and paper or online document).
2. Prompt learners to consider their strongest relationships in each of the three Social Capital categories: People who are like them (bonds), people who are different from

them in some meaningful way (bridges), and people in power (links). Often learners don't know who they know. As they make their lists, encourage them to think deeply about the connections they have. What sort of careers do their parents have? Their aunts and uncles? Friends of the family? Learners can also use the Tracker as a rolodex, capturing key information so that they can follow up when they may need something like a letter of recommendation.

3. Encourage learners to ask their parents to review their lists and help them add any names they may have forgotten.

4. Check in with each learner individually throughout the year to revisit progress and support areas of need.

5. As you bring in outside experts and community members to your learning projects, create the expectation that learners should be capturing the person's information and expanding their Tracker.

The role of the learner is to

1. Consider who they already know, and make a list of names in each of the three categories to keep record of their strongest relationships.

2. Pay attention to gaps in each of the three Social Capital categories and devise a strategy for remedying the imbalances. For example, if learners are lacking in linking relationships, they may benefit from a mentor or apprenticeship. If learners are lacking in bridging relationships, they can work on a group project with learners they haven't worked with yet. If learners are lacking in bonds, they may join a club based on one of their interests.

3. Create plans for intentionally nourishing the relationships that matter most to them. What actions can each learner take to develop and grow relationships in each of the three Social Capital categories?

What you need:
- ◆ Paper and a pen, or a Google/Word document
- ◆ Time scheduled for learners to list their relationships
- ◆ Check-ins to follow up on progress

The gist:
With a Social Capital Tracker, learners know they are supported. This visual representation brings their social network into clear view. It's important to remember that all learners come from different backgrounds. Their existing connections may already include people in power, or they may not. Some learners may not know anyone different from them, or for example in the case of an international student or newcomer, may not feel connected to anyone like them. Educators can get to know their learners, help them reflect on the strengths and holes in their social networks, and provide support and opportunities as they seek to grow their relationships. A Social Capital Tracker provides actionable steps to learners and their Dream Teams by showcasing the gaps that exist in a learner's relationship network. This is a helpful, easy tool we can use as we work to surround each and every learner with multiple caring adults.

Apprenticeships

System Element: Community Practices and School Culture

Biggest Ripple Effect: Bridges and Partnerships (with companies, professionals, etc.), Roles (to crowdsource connections to professionals), and Assessment (to guide learners and employers to reflect on the value of the experience)

What it is and why:
Apprenticeships are real-world work experiences. Learners apprentice under a career professional in a field of their choosing. Apprenticeships offer learners an opportunity an experience to work with someone in a career they are interested in (or try

something outside of their comfort zone, even if they aren't interested in pursuing a career in that field). Some schools have staff dedicated to facilitating connections between students and trade masters, but there is value in equipping and empowering young people to seek out and secure their own apprenticeships.

During apprenticeships, learners are able to get real, hands-on, project-based work experience. They are able to investigate what they want to do or not do. It's a way for learners to jump into the day-to-day of various professions early, so by the time they graduate they have a better understanding of their calling and are able to narrow down their choices and continue to build their social network before jumping into the real world.

How do to it:

The role of the educator is to:
1. Introduce the idea of Apprenticeships to learners and prompt them to consider their fields of interest.
2. Meet with learners to help them make social connections and consider how they may find compelling opportunities.
3. Tap your own network and engage parents at your school to consider taking on an apprentice.
4. Help learners communicate with potential field experts to propose their idea for an apprenticeship.
5. Once a learner has landed an apprenticeship, guide them to consider the questions they have, what they want to learn, and the outcomes they hope to experience.

The role of the learner is to:
1. Determine areas of interest for potential apprenticeships.
2. Connect with people in power, either within their own social networks or in the networks surrounding their own, to propose the idea of an apprenticeship.

3. Consider the goals, questions, and curiosities they have within this field of interest.
4. Show up for the apprenticeship, engage, and reflect on what they learn.
5. Report about the experience and outcomes.

What you need:

♦ Time to prompt learners to consider possible apprenticeship opportunities.

♦ Time to meet with learners individually to support their endeavors.

♦ Leverage your own social networks to help learners find apprenticeships.

♦ Process or protocol to provide boundaries for off-campus experiences (Cristo Rey Jesuit School has an inspiring Corporate Work Study Program. Learn more at www. cristoreyatlanta.org).

♦ Deadlines and expectations for learners to submit final deliverables.

The Gist:

Because learners are children, they haven't had enough time to develop a rich, diverse social network for themselves. Some learners inherit robust communities from their families of origin. Others do not. Learners need not only real-world practice in order to discover their calling, but also relationships with people of influence to support them in and beyond school. As educators, we can help resource learners with not only the skills and knowledge they need, but the relationships that will help them succeed.

Mentoring
System Element: Roles

Biggest Ripple Effect: Schedules and Routines (to make time), Community Practices and School Culture (to cultivate and celebrate mentoring relationships).

What it is and Why:
The true richness of a learner-led environment is the wisdom that resides in the learners themselves. In many school settings, learners have little opportunity or incentive to share this wisdom with their peers. What if, instead, a key part of being at school was mentoring your peers? Mentoring can look like a lot of things. It could be subject-related, with older students mentoring younger learners in math, writing, and other fields. It could be interpersonal, where more mature learners "coach up" younger students in regards to leadership and citizenship. The key is to give it a structure, incentivize it, and celebrate it. Mentorships pair older and younger learners together so students can lead, connect, and learn from each other. Learners can choose their own mentors or request help from an educator to find a good match. Mentorships can last as long as learners like. We encourage learners to connect with multiple mentors throughout the year to grow their social networks, expand their thinking, and diversify their experiences in leading and being led by their peers.

How to do it:
1. Create a clear process. What does mentoring look like? How are mentors selected? What's the format? What are the accountability systems? A good mentoring program is unlikely to happen on its own. Learners will need structures and systems to utilize in order to grow in the skills of mentorship, with lots of coaching along the way.
2. Help facilitate connections among learners who need support in finding a mentor or mentee.

3. Provide a safe space for both mentors and mentees to request counsel, feedback, or support in navigating the mentorship.
4. Offer suggestions for how learners can get the most out of their mentorships. Prompt self-reflective questions like: "What do I want to learn from an older learner?" "What do I have to offer or teach a younger learner?"
5. Incentivize it. If I'm a learner, I may be more invested in doing my own work and meeting my own goals than helping someone else. Some schools create mentoring requirements that learners must meet before they can complete their learning plans.
6. Structure time for learners to meet with their mentors.
7. Celebrate it. Recognize learners who are world-class mentors. Facilitate opportunities for students to publicly share gratitude for peers who helped them.

What you need:
   ◆ A clear mentorship process. Document the constraints and expectations of your mentorship protocol.
   ◆ Time in the schedule to introduce mentorships to learners and prompt them to consider who they may want to learn from or offer support to.
   ◆ Use Check-ins as a way to explore mentorships with individual learners.

The gist:
Mentorships offer ways for learners to connect with each other and grow together. Within mentorships, learners are able to practice leadership skills, communication, collaboration, and empathy. Mentorships facilitate robust personal relationships among learners. They create opportunities for learners from every grade to intersect with and encourage each other.

An example:
Northern Cass School District has a program called Luminaries. Made up of volunteer juniors and seniors, Luminaries receive training in giving high-quality peer feedback and take turns being stationed in the library. Students from any class or grade level can schedule time to meet with a Luminary and receive one-on-one coaching and feedback on their work.

Outside Experts
System Element: Roles

Biggest Ripple Effect: Assessment (guide experts to give real world feedback), Schedules and Routines (to make time), and Curriculum (embed experts into classroom and projects).

What it is and why:
The role of traditional educators is to be an evaluator of student work. In a learner-led environment, educators create multiple feedback channels for learners to receive feedback on their work. One of the ways we bring that experience to self-directed learners is to invite actual experts in a certain field to give students, either individually or in groups, direct feedback on how they can improve what they're working on. External experts are masters of a trade, skill, or particular field. Experts invited into a self-directed learning environment not only share about what they do and what it took for them to get there, but also review student work and offer feedback for improvement. Additionally, bringing in external experts provides learners the opportunity to expand their social capital. Learners can follow up with experts for apprenticeship opportunities or to consider joining their Dream Teams.

How to do it:

The role of the educator is to:
1. Find an expert relevant to what your learners are studying. You can call on people from your own network, engage the school community, or reach out to specific field experts students want to learn from. Technology has made it possible to connect with experts from around the world.
2. Invite external experts to visit the school, make a request for your learners to visit their workplace, or connect virtually.
3. Facilitate dialog and encourage learners to share their own work to receive real-world feedback. Encourage learners to ask: How did we do? Did we knock it out of the park or not? What can we do differently next time?

The role of the learner is to:
1. Name the experts or professional fields they want to learn more about.
2. Add the expert to their Social Capital Tracker.
3. Ask the expert questions about their profession and what it took to get there.
4. Share work with experts to receive relevant feedback.

What you need:
- ◆ A diverse social network for calling in experts.
- ◆ Scheduled time to visit an expert's place of work, or to welcome them into the classroom.
- ◆ Current, relevant student work for experts to respond to.

An example:
"One year, during a presidential election, we invited several politicians and other experts in the field of politics to visit with our

learners. During this opportunity, learners were interviewed by the political experts, not the other way around! We had learners as young as 5 years old on stage responding to questions about topics like recycling, trade policies, and world peace. These experts had real-world experience in politics, so learners were able to learn firsthand what political life is really like. What better practice for preparing for the real world?"

The gist:
Experts are resources for students to learn more about a particular subject and build relationships with people in power. Learners are able to interview experts on their knowledge, get to know them, and receive direct feedback. This gives learners the chance to glean wisdom from someone in the field, build a relationship with a person of influence, and see what it takes to get where they've gotten. As a school leader, strengthen your connection with outside experts by sending follow-up thank you notes, inviting them to school events, reaching out to them if you need sponsorships, and asking them how you can add value to their work.

Shout-Outs
System Elements: Community Practices and School Culture

Biggest Ripple Effect: Schedules and Routines (to make time)

What it is and why:
One way to strengthen relationships in your classroom is to have a regular practice of learners sharing gratitude for one another. Shout Outs is an intentional block of time where learners and educators gather together to call attention to the positive qualities and behaviors they've witnessed in one another. This is an important moment. It is a time for the class to recognize those who have done outstanding things, like helping a fellow learner

with a math problem, solving a conflict, or displaying leadership. Shout Outs is a way of intentionally celebrating one another. Shout Outs organically incentivize collaboration, kindness, and leadership. They give learners the opportunity to feel seen, celebrated, and valued by their peers and educators. Learners look forward to this time. They want to hear what they've done well, and they want to share the love with their friends. The cadence of this is flexible. For subject area teachers who have multiple classes in a day, maybe this is a weekly practice. For teachers with the same students every day, maybe Shout Outs is a routine end of day practice.

How do to it:

The role of the educator is to:
1. Schedule time for learners to call out the good they've seen in one another (the cadence is up to you!).
2. Participate! Share the positive behaviors you witnessed during the day.

The role of the learner is to:
1. Shout someone out, give a celebratory announcement, or appreciate what someone did.
   1. Encourage learners to think through: Who really stepped up today? Who went out of their way to make me feel like I belong? Who helped me in math? Who did an awesome job of sweeping the classroom?
2. Reflect on the positive feedback they receive.
   1. One benefit to Shout Outs is that learners get to see what they've done to help others throughout the day. They see their strengths and have the chance to feel seen and celebrated. Encourage learners to receive and reflect on the positive qualities others seem to notice in them.

What you need:
- ◆ Time in the schedule (we recommend 10–15 minutes)
- ◆ A protocol. Without structure, Shout Outs could easily become a popularity contest where the same learners are celebrated or friends only shout out each other. There are a variety of facilitation techniques out there (we're big fans of Liberating Structures menu of routines. Learn more at www.liberatingstructures.com). Experiment with a few to maximize the engagement and ensure equity in the process.

Parent Coffees

System Element: Community Practices and School Culture

Biggest Ripple Effect: Roles (school leaders see themselves as edu-cators of parents and caregivers, not just of teachers), Schedules and Routines (time for it), and Facilities (space for it)

What it is and Why:
Parents and caregivers in your community will have various degrees of connection and interaction with the school. One way to strengthen the bond between school leaders, educators, and parents/caregivers is to host regular meet-ups. We host monthly Parent Coffees at our school, and this is a great way to build community, create a safe space for dialogue and feedback, and deepen the understanding of parents/caregivers around our approach to learner-led education.

How to do it:
- ◆ Get it on the schedule. Go ahead and schedule Parent Coffees for the school year and share the times and dates with your school families. Schedule it for a high-impact time when most parents will be available (we've found a lot of success with scheduling right after morning

drop-off). You may also want to make a few of these meetings virtual and could schedule during the lunch hour to appeal to parents/caregivers who might not be available in the mornings.

♦ Have a topic. Create an intentional adult learning experience around a facet of your school. This is an opportunity to share insights into the work of the school (and the philosophy behind that) as well as overlap with broader conversations about parenting and education. (A good way to decide on topics is to poll parents for questions they have or topics they would like to explore further).

♦ Provide lots of space for conversation. The goal of a Parent Coffee is to deepen the relationships parents have with each other and the school.

♦ Create a safe, low-risk environment for parents/caregivers to share feedback or concerns.

♦ Cultivate connections between new parents and returning families.

♦ End with gratitude and celebration.

Conflict Resolution

System Element: Community Practices and School Culture

Biggest Ripple Effect: Roles (training staff to mediate)

What it is and Why:
All schools have some mechanism for conflict resolution. Some are systematic and fail to cultivate deeper relationships. An intentional approach to guiding learners to address and work through conflict with their peers will cultivate stronger relationships among students and create a stronger culture within the school.

How to do it:

In Chapter 7, we'll provide a deeper dive into guiding learners to create their own rules of systems of governance. Here, though, we'll focus specifically on a relationships-based approach to conflict resolution. Here are some frameworks to keep in mind:

The educator's role is to:

- Be an impartial facilitator. Create a clear, transparent process that is fair to all parties.
- Create a space in your classroom where conflict resolution can happen. Some schools have a Peace Table where learners go to work through a conflict.
- Have a protocol for learners to follow. One option is SBIF (situation, behavior, impact, future):
  - *Situation*: Have the offended party specify where and when the incident happened. For example, "During PE yesterday, ..."
  - *Behavior*: Have the offended party specify what the other learner did or said to hurt or offend them. For example, "...you taunted me for losing..."
  - *Impact*: Have the offended party specify the impact that the other learner's actions/behavior had on them. For example, "...I was embarrassed and hurt..."
  - *Future*: Have the offended party point to how they would like the other learner to (1) start to rebuild trust, and (2) act in the future. For example, "...I would still like to play with you, if you're sorry for what happened and won't taunt me again."
- Guide the other party to practice active listening and to respond by saying "I hear you saying..." This keeps the focus on the incident and not on overlapping social dynamics.

- Guide all learners involved to *own what they need to own*. Chances are, multiple students fell short of class agreements and expectations. Invite each learner to take responsibility for their actions and come to a collaborative decision about what needs to happen next.
- The outcome of the conflict resolution should be clear (all parties understand it), actionable (all parties know how to make amends), and time-bound (future actions aren't left vague).
- Follow up with all parties to see how things are going.
- Build the capacity of student leaders to facilitate conflict resolution. Educators can and should still oversee the process to ensure fairness and equity, but "handing off" the facilitation to learners builds the muscle of the community to address and solve their own conflicts.
- Conflict Resolution is especially powerful (and tricky to navigate) across lines of difference. How do educators and school leaders create a Conflict Resolution protocol that allows learners to navigate deep differences (i.e., racial, religious, or cultural)? It's complex and the ideas here are insufficient, but here are some tips we've learned:
  - Consistently interrogate the organization and its systems for bias. Get feedback from the learners, the staff, the parents/caregivers, and the community. As a school leader, be humble and willing to learn. Model the growth mindset you would like to see in the wider school community.
  - Protect every student's sense of identity, safety, and belonging. Each learner should know that you as the school leader or educator have their back and want the best for them. Frequently monitor the culture (schoolwide and class by class) via Belonging Surveys or something similar.

- ◆ When facilitating Conflict Resolution across lines of difference, the skills/mindsets to focus on for learners are *active listening*, *empathy*, and mutual *sense-making*. This approach has at its end goal mutual understanding. Each learner hears and *understands* where the other is coming from.
- ◆ Conflict Resolution between individuals may be an indicator that larger conversations need to happen with the whole class on navigating specific lines of difference. One-on-one Conflict Resolutions will be strengthened if there are class-wide conversations and a larger focus on building a culture where everyone feels a deep sense of belonging.

We mention many more learner-led Conflict Resolution techniques later in the book, but one resource worth checking it out that is gaining momentum in public school districts is Student-Led Restorative Practices (https://studentledrp.org).

Conclusion

Building strong networks of relationships is key to cultivating a culture of interdependent, self-directed learning. Researchers argue that a student's relationship network is among the strongest predictors of educational outcomes. Researchers have found that social capital contributes to a number of educational achievements, including but not limited to much lower dropout rates, improved adaptation pathways, foreign language acquisition, higher grade point averages, and lower levels of misbehavior. We know that the strength and breadth of a learner's social network is a key indicator of their flourishing, in school and beyond (Putnam, 2000). A leader's role is to guide team members, parents, and learners through meaningful experiences that build each of their capacities to grow and maintain relationships.

References

Fisher, J. (2020, February 14). *How to get a job often comes down to one elite personal asset, and many people still don't realize it*. CNBC. https://www.cnbc.com/2019/12/27/how-to-get-a-job-often-comes-down-to-one-elite-personal-asset.html

Greenfield Dream Teams - the Exchange. (2023, April 14). The Exchange. https://exchange.transcendeducation.org/models/greenfield-dream-teams/

Lin, Nan. (2002) *Social Capital: A Theory of Social Structure and Action*. Cambridge University Press.

Putnam, R. D. (2000). *Bowling alone: The collapse and revival of American community*. Touchstone Books/Simon & Schuster. https://doi.org/10.1145/358916.361990

Waldinger, R. and Schulz, M. (2023). *The Good Life: Lessons from the World's Longest Scientific Study on Happiness*. Simon and Schuster.

3

Focusing on the Whole Child

There are many competing (and sometimes conflicting) opinions about what the main focus of education should be. Some would argue that school is primarily about cultivating skills and knowledge necessary for a career. Others see education as a means for personal growth, where learners grow in understanding of themselves and their world. Some, like John Dewey, argued that education was for social reproduction. We raise up the next generation to carry society into the future. Wrapped up in these debates about education are relevant themes to this book. Is education primarily for the individual learner, or is it primarily a public good? How much of education should be standardized and systematized and how much should be customizable? How should the views and desires of parents shape the purpose of individual schools? How about the views and desires of learners?

You may come to this book from any number of viewpoints about the *why* of education. We're not going to take on the whole debate, but we'll carve out a small space of the discussion. We

DOI: 10.4324/9781003489894-3

have a strong point of view that one of the motivating *whys* of school should be cultivating in every child the skills and knowledge to make meaningful choices about their own lives. Yes, that will touch on things like preparing for college or the workforce. But it's not *just* that. The lessons, mindsets, and habits cultivated in school aren't just for academia. And they're not siloed to a career path. They touch on every aspect of human life. A goal for schools should be to cultivate flourishing humans. To do that, school leaders will need to focus not just on the curriculum and systems that shape students. They will need to embrace human-centered design that takes into account the whole person.

In this chapter, we'll lay out some techniques that leaders can utilize to grow the capacities of their teams in this regard. Many education and teacher training programs focus on the nuts and bolts of lesson plans or the specifics of content disciplines. Creating a school that cultivates flourishing for the whole child will take intentionality and will probably require additional learning opportunities for the adults on your team.

A Story

An interesting experiment of employing self-directed pedagogies in a public school began in Jefferson County, Colorado in 1970. A group of parents approached the school district with a request to open an alternative school option. Rick Posner (2009) tells the story of the school in his book *Lives of Passion, School of Hope*. The school, the Jefferson County Open School (often just referred to as the Open School), would focus on "developing the whole person," not just academics (p. 10). The staff and students co-created the school in the early 1970s, putting forth the following goals for their space:

- ◆ Rediscover the joy of learning
- ◆ Engage in the search for meaning in your life

- ◆ Adapt to the world that is
- ◆ Prepare for the world that might be
- ◆ Help create the world that ought to be

Alongside these goals, the school had five learner outcomes. Each learner was "expected to become an effective communicator, a complex thinker, a responsible citizen, an ethical person, and a quality worker" (p. 10). Those are lofty goals and outcomes. How did the Open School plan to achieve them?

The first step was the positioning of everyone involved as a *learner first and foremost*. Parents, teachers, administrators, students, and janitors were all perceived as a community of learners. Secondly, the school functioned on a system of democracy. Students were represented proportionally on a governing council, and the council decided such decisions as hiring/firing personnel, course offerings, and the curriculum used. Third, the Open School is centered on self-directed pedagogies and cultivates self-directed skills in teachers and students (remember, everyone is a *learner* first). The school identified the following quadrants of learning:

TABLE 3.1 Adapted from Posner (2009, p. 13)

	Formal Learning	*Informal Learning*
In School	Planned learning in-school	Unplanned learning in-school
	Formal learning that occurs in classrooms, lecture halls, laboratories, workshops, presentations, etc.	Informal learning that occurs in spontaneous discussions, socialization in the halls and cafeteria, or unexpected events in formal settings such as a laboratory project that does not go as planned, etc.
Out of School	Planned learning out-of-school	Unplanned learning out-of-school
	Learning that occurs at conferences, field trips, internships, apprenticeships, family trips, work, etc.	Learning that occurs through time spent with friends and family, travel without formal agendas, sports activities, playing, reading, etc.

So, for the Open School, learning activities like lectures are not contrary to self-directed learning, but fit within it. Each high school student is assigned an advisor that assists that student in building a Mutually Agreed-upon Program (MAP) for their high school career. The MAP may involve a web of traditionally-styled courses that focus heavy on lectures, collaborative labs and workshops, internships and apprenticeships outside of school, and other learning activities. To graduate at The Open School, learners must complete six "passages"—self-directed projects in the areas of creativity, practical skills, logical inquiry, adventure, career exploration, and global awareness (p. 15). No passage looks the same for any two students. The Open School does not give grades or offer traditional transcripts. Graduates must write their own narrative transcript, documenting their learning journey at The Open School and making an argument as to why they are ready for life in the real world. Posner (2009) noted that 91% of alumni surveyed had attended college.

Techniques

Mission and Values

System Element: Vision

Biggest Ripple Effect: Assessment (reporting on whole-child growth)

What it is and Why:
Your mission is your North Star. It's your reason for doing what you do. Usually, a school's mission will be summed up in a succinct statement, putting a clear stake in the ground for *why* the school exists and what it is aiming to do. Along with this mission statement, founders and leaders will list out their values and design principles. These provide a framework for building out the school model. They also serve as a type of filter. Every time a

new decision is being considered, leaders will weigh the choices against their mission, values, and design principles to see which options are most aligned. Since so much hinges on the mission and values of the school, it's up to you as a school leader to be intentional, thoughtful, and inclusive in creating these guiding principles. (Quick note: In wayfinding, the North Star is never the destination. Instead, it's a way for travelers to orient themselves to where they are and take stock of where they are headed. Likewise, your mission and vision are meant to be tools that aid you in your day-to-day work by guiding you to reflect on where you are and where you are going).

How to do it:

There are entire books and courses dedicated to crafting compelling mission statements. We're not going to be comprehensive here. Rather, we're going to offer some questions and processes to consider.

1. First, think about your own why. Why are you in the position you are in? What are you seeking to accomplish? Why your own personal mission or purpose statement.
2. Next, what makes your school unique? Make a list of compelling reasons your school should exist.
3. Then, go to the community. In the previous chapter, we provided relational tools for engaging with parents/caregivers, your team, and other stakeholders in the community. Talk to people in the neighborhood. Do research. Practice active listening. Hear from the community their hopes and fears as it relates to their children's education. Record these findings.
4. Weigh your personal mission statement against the notes from your community outreach. Where's the greatest alignment? The greatest disconnect? What adjustments need to be made?

5. Draft a version 1.0 of a mission statement and list of values. Get feedback from other school leaders, education designers, and the community. Revise as needed.

6. Use your mission and values to recruit the right team. You want buy-in from your staff into the mission of the school. If there is a disconnect, you'll either need to get the buy-in through intentional professional development or risk hampering the mission by building a team that lacks alignment.

7. Have continual feedback from the community, including staff and learners, on these guiding principles. Be quick to listen, but slow to make any drastic changes to your North Star.

The bottom line:

There's a good chance you read this technique and thought, "We already have a mission statement. We're all set!" Before you move on, though, deeply reflect on your current mission statement. Can you name your mission statement off the top of your head? Can your educators, parents, and learners? Does your mission statement influence how you make decisions or do your work on a daily basis? If not, consider tweaking it.

Portrait of a Graduate

System Element: Vision

Biggest Ripple Effect: Curriculum, Assessment, and Pedagogy (measuring and teaching what we care about most)

What it is and Why:

A Portrait of a Graduate is a snapshot of the skills, knowledge, and mindsets that graduates of your school are expected to master. This will be connected to the mission and values of your institution, and will also be a framework and filter for the rest of your school design. The Portrait of a Graduate is an answer to the question, "What do we want to be true of our young people when they leave our school?" Below are questions and processes to consider.

How to do it:
1. First, step back. If you have kids, think about what you want to be true of their own school experience. If you don't have kids, put yourself in the shoes of a parent. List out the skills, knowledge, and mindsets you think are crucial (in terms of academics, character traits, and career readiness) for young people to have mastered by the time they leave your school.
2. Look to the future. What skills, knowledge, and mindsets will be crucial five, ten, or fifteen years in the future?
3. Research and compare. Hold up your Portrait of a Graduate to other schools. Look up exemplars (we've provided The Forest School's below). Consider what education designers are arguing for in terms of graduate outcomes.
4. Go to the community. Again, buy-in is key. Ask your community to give feedback on the Portrait of a Graduate. Host a design sprint. Take lots of notes.
5. Organize a version 1.0 of a Portrait of a Graduate. Create categories to help group the outcomes in a way that is easy to see and understand.
6. Get feedback on your Portrait of a Graduate. Revise as needed.
7. Have continual feedback from the community, including staff and learners, on the Portrait of a Graduate. Be quick to listen, but slow to make any drastic changes. The world is rapidly changing and chances are you will need to tweak this list over the lifetime of your school.
8. Allow for customization. It's important that learners don't just see the Portrait of a Graduate as another set of expectations set for them by someone else. Leave spaces in your Portrait for learners to add and define their own competencies.

Portrait of a Graduate

Learn to Be	Learn to Do	Learn to Learn	Learn to Live Together
• Flourishing • Purpose • Resourcefulness • Growth mindset • Gratitude	• Storytelling • Creativity • Entrepreneurship • Design thinking • Goal setting & reflection	• Learning science • Math • English • Civilization • Science	• Collaboration • Empathy • Trust • Cross-cultural competence • Social capital

FIGURE 3.1 The Forest School's Portrait of a Graduate.

Redefining the Role of Educator

System Element: Roles

Biggest Ripple Effect: Onboarding (hiring and training teachers for a revised set of educator competencies)

What it is and Why:

There is a dramatic difference in the role of the educator in learner-led spaces. Teachers in traditional settings are content experts, evaluators, and managers. Educators in self-directed schools are more often called guides, facilitators, or mentors. It is important for the school leader to clearly understand and define the educator's role, specifically calling out how it differs from traditional teaching, create ways to coach their team on this re-envisioned role, and provide ample opportunities for professional growth. Many learner-led environments have guides, not teachers. A guide has four distinct roles:

1. Mentor and Coach: A guide is a role model that *showcases* self-directed learning in all they do. They work to

inspire and equip young people to take responsibility for their own learning. They support learners' personal and academic growth. They monitor a learner's progress and coach them along the way.

2. Gamemaker, Curator, and Facilitator: A guide creates fun, engaging learning activities. They design for deep learning, with an eye for how to motivate learners. They find and curate resources (human and material) that learners can utilize in their projects.

3. Leader and Manager: Even in self-directed spaces, a guide helps captain the ship. Their main role is to ensure safety and equity in the classroom. They oversee the systems and operations at work in the class, holding the learners accountable to the promises they have made to themselves and each other.

4. Networker and Communicator: A guide is well-skilled at relationship building. This happens first in the classroom, where a guide works to build strong trust with each and every learner. Guides also work to help their learners strengthen their own social capital by creating a classroom of "porous walls" and helping learners connect with a diverse network of caring adults. Guides also work alongside learners to keep parents/caregivers abreast of a learner's learning goals and progress on those goals.

How to do it:
1. Get specific. What *is* the role of an educator in your school? How is it the same and different from the job of a traditional teacher? Clearly articulate the knowledge, craft, and skills educators in your space are expected to cultivate.

2. Hire right. Look for candidates that buy into your vision and have the requisite skill sets. Many times, traditionally trained teachers are a hindrance to self-directed learning, as they have a lot of *unlearning* to do around what the role

of an educator is. A key look-for: how self-directed is the person you are hiring? Are they able to lead their own learning journey?

3. Provide ample support and opportunities for professional growth. Build in multiple processes for onboarding, continuing professional growth, coaching, and reflection. For most teachers coming from traditional colleges of education, the concept of "guiding" will be new and quite different (and contrary to) their traditional training. Likewise, teachers who have been in the classroom for many years will need time, coaching, and space to "unlearn" many of their habits.

4. Be nimble. Chances are, as your school grows, you'll make slight changes to the role of the educator. Take a growth mindset, learn along the way, and be willing to adjust the role as needed.

Mastery-Based Transcripts

System Element: Assessment

Biggest Ripple Effect: Community Practices and School Culture (to provide rituals for mastery-based learning and sharing); Tech and Tech Infrastructure (to visualize and report learning)

What it is and Why:
This chapter is all about "focusing on the whole child." A key way to do that is to utilize a transcript process that allows college admissions and HR departments a chance to see a wide snapshot of your graduates. Most students in this country earn As and Bs on their transcripts (Craft, 2023). GPAs don't really tell a story about *who* the learner is and what they've accomplished. The Forest School became the first school in the nation to pilot a mastery transcript created by the Mastery Transcript Consortium (Mastery Transcript Consortium, 2024). Our graduates have used this transcript to

gain admittance to their first choice colleges, all without submitting grades or GPAs. Here's how to design your own mastery-based transcript.

How to do it:

1. Use your Portrait of a Graduate as a list of all the competencies your students must master.
2. Clearly define the competencies in easy-to-understand language and create a single-point rubric for each one (example provided below).
3. Design Signature Learning Experiences (we give guidance on these later) to cultivate the skills, mindsets, and knowledge listed in the Portrait of a Graduate and allow students to gain plentiful practice at these competencies.
4. Guide students to begin compiling evidence (in and out of school) that they can one day present as evidence of mastery.
5. Create a flexible assessment protocol for learners to present evidence of mastery (see the technique of Practicals in Chapter 10 for guidance).
6. Consider contracting with the Mastery Transcript Consortium (www.mastery.org) as a way to host, collect, and present evidence of mastery in compelling reports.

Holistic Progress Reports

System Element: Assessment

Biggest Ripple Effect: Community Practices and School Culture

What it is and Why:

Like transcripts, most progress reports utilized by schools give students semi-arbitrary markings like As and Bs to demonstrate academic progress. These reports provide little insight into how a student collaborates with others, how they problem solve, or what their strengths and areas of growth are. What if, instead, progress reports offered clear snapshots of how the student was growing and progressing (holistically) as measured against the Portrait of a Graduate?

How to do it:

1. Choose what competencies you're measuring. Use your Portrait of a Graduate as a guide. At The Forest School, we take a scaffolding approach. Our youngest learners focus on a handful of competencies. They take on more and more as they move through Elementary and Middle grades. Then, in High School, they have to show mastery of all of our graduate outcomes. This approach is also used by the school system in Logan County, Kentucky.

2. Choose how you will measure. If you utilize e-learning platforms like Khan Academy, these can be a part of the metric. We use a host of diagnostic tools (which we explore in detail in Chapter 10), including Practicals, Badges, and public exhibitions.

3. Get learners involved. A key skill in self-directed learning is the ability to evaluate your own progress. Create a template that learners can complete themselves, with places to log their progress in all subjects, post examples of their best work, reflect on their learning, and create a plan of action for what's next.

4. Provide parents/caregivers a transparent view into the work of their children, but keep the learner in the driver's seat. Any conferences with the teachers and parents should involve the learner, and the learner themselves should lead the conference.

5. Don't forget to celebrate. Each child is much more than their "progress" in academics. Highlight growth you've seen. How has the learner shown leadership,

collaboration, kindness, and empathy? Celebrate those with the learner and their caregivers.

6. Provide parents language to use and questions to ask. Most parents are products of the traditional education system. They will need coaching in how to discuss school with their children. When we send out any version of a progress report or learning update, we include questions parents can use to engage with their child.

Customizable Learning Plans

System Element: Curriculum, Assessment, and Pedagogy

Biggest Ripple Effect: Roles (training teachers to manage the quality of learning through multiple channels)

What it is and Why:
Schools should not be seen as factories. Unfortunately, that's how they're often formulated and designed. Students are often treated as products moving across conveyor belts, "content" being downloaded into their brains along the way. This view of education promotes conformity; at the end of the day, every student is on the hook for the same arbitrary knowledge base. What if, though, each learner had a say in what they were learning (i.e., outcomes) and the pathway they took to learn it (i.e., curriculum)? At many learner-led schools, each learner not only *can* but is *strongly encouraged* to modify their learning plan. Learners, in concert with caregivers and educators, create their own units of study, identify the resources they use, the milestones they'll meet, and determine how they will demonstrate mastery.

How to do it:
1. Using your Portrait of a Graduate, identify all the *required* skills, mindsets, and knowledge all of your learners are on the hook for.

2. Guide learners to create a learning plan that encompasses all the required competencies *but leaves room for self-selected courses.*

3. Create a protocol for learners to add, subtract, or change their learning plans. At The Forest School, we provide learners with a checklist to consider as they create a new course. New courses need to be signed off on by educators and caregivers. (Sometimes this can be an earned privilege: new learners that show that they can meet their learning goals are given greater and greater autonomy on their learning plans).

4. Create a school that has "porous walls." Provide lots of opportunities for learners to hear about, try out, and engage a wide range of interests that they can pursue *where they are* by tapping the expertise of the community.

5. Celebrate learners that pursue their interests!

Multicultural, Diverse-by-Design Environments

System Element: Vision

Biggest Ripple Effect: Community Practices and School Culture (celebrating learning across lines of difference); Roles (hiring diverse staff and recruiting a diverse student body); Onboarding (training teachers to do this well)

What it is and Why:
Part of focusing on the whole child is creating an environment that sees and celebrates their authentic selves. All children, regardless of race, religion, gender, school background, or income levels, should feel a deep sense of belonging. This doesn't happen accidentally. It takes intentionality and strategic thinking on the part of school leaders and educators. This will be more challenging for schools with heterogeneous populations. There are many kinds of diversity, and your role as

school leader is to create abundant opportunities for learners to work and learn across lines of difference.

How to do it:

1. With lots of feedback from the community and education designers, craft language around your school's approach to cultivating a multicultural, diverse environment.

2. Research your community. Where are you situated? What's the demographic breakdown?

3. Set target goals that are in alignment with the demographics of your community.

4. Build relationships with gatekeepers in the community. At The Forest School, we found that connecting with local centers of worship and organizations (like the NAACP) were crucial in sharing the opportunity of our school with a variety of groups.

5. Mitigate the financial barrier. Cost is one of the key factors that limits a family's access to a learner-led school environment. If you're a school leader in the private sector, you will need to prioritize how to assist and support families that can't afford the tuition. Offer flexible tuition. Research the resources of your state (in Georgia, schools can use the state's Apogee program to direct tax dollars toward our scholarships). Explore philanthropic avenues. Do the work needed to make your learning environment accessible to people from any income level.

6. Celebrate cultural differences. Every year, each learner in our Pre-K class invites their parents and caregivers to come in and share their story. They share genealogies, favorite foods, and cultural celebrations. They learn at a young age that their *whole self* is welcome and celebrated here. This echoes throughout the older classrooms as well. As a school leader, find ways to recognize and celebrate the diversity of life experiences present in your school.

Celebrating Wins

System Element: Community Practices and School Culture

Biggest Ripple Effect: Communications (publicly sharing what gets celebrated)

What it is and Why:

There's an old saying, "You cultivate what you celebrate." So, what is celebrated in your school? Many schools celebrate academics (Honor Roll, Dean's List, Advanced/Gifted labels), but that is a very narrow view of what a child is, who they are, and what they are contributing to the community. As a leader, how can you make *celebration* a key cornerstone of your school? Here are some ideas:

How to do it:

1. Start at the top. How do you celebrate your team? Be intentional about "shouting out" your team members as they go about the hard (often unseen and uncelebrated) work of education.

2. Create rituals. Build celebrations into the rhythms and routines of your school. Put them on the calendar. Celebrate learners throughout the year for a variety of reasons (making progress on their learning goals, exemplifying the characteristics of your Portrait of a Graduate, holding others accountable, owning their own mistakes, etc.).

3. Make space for gratitude, every day. Throughout the book, we highlight techniques like Shout Outs. Educators can use a variety of processes and protocols to facilitate, but the gist of this time is to give learners the ability to name and celebrate the actions and attitudes of their peers.

Circles

System Elements: Curriculum, Pedagogy, and Assessment

Biggest Ripple Effect: Roles (training); Schedules and Routines (making time)

What it is and Why:
The purpose of Circles is to increase levels of connection and strengthen relationships among learners and to advance their personal, interpersonal, and community growth (Valor, 2022). We've adapted our Circle process from Valor' Compass Model (www.poweredbycompass.org). Think of Circles as an intentionally created safe space for the community to connect, allow learners to share pieces of their identity, and provide an avenue for conflict resolution when appropriate.

How to do it:
1. Have a clear process. We recommend researching Valor's Compass Model. Whatever template you find to facilitate group social/emotional learning, make it your own and align it with your systems.
2. Model it with your team. Before you start using something like Circles in your classrooms, take time to use it with your staff. This will not only aid the cultural building of your team, it will give them practice experiencing Circles before they step into the role of facilitator.
3. Put it on the schedule. Class schedules get real busy, real fast. There's a ton of awesome stuff we want learners to experience. Often, social-emotional learning work like Circles gets left out. Determine a consistent rhythm for Circles and carve out time on the schedule.
4. Learn as you go. Your approach to cultivating community in your school and classrooms will change over time.

Transdisciplinary Project-Based Learning
System Element: Curriculum, Pedagogy, and Assessment

Biggest Ripple Effect: Roles (training); Onboarding; Bridges and
  Partnerships (for authentic project-based learning)

What it is and Why:
In traditional classrooms, a student's day is mostly "siloed"
into disparate subjects. They go to Math class. Then Science. So
on and so forth. That type of learning does not mimic the real
world. In work and in life, we approach projects, problems, and
questions that are multidisciplinary by nature. We might have
to tap into our math, science, and communication skills to successfully navigate a project. What if schools provided young
people the same opportunities? At a 1996 convening, UNSECO
highlighted the need for a "transdisciplinary vision" for education in an information age (UNESCO, 1997). Most Industrial
Age school models have been slow to move away from siloed
coursework. Many schools utilize transdisciplinary project-
based learning to provide learners opportunities to utilize various skill sets and demonstrate mastery of subject matter. Here's
how you might consider implementing these projects in your
classroom.

How to do it:
1. Start with a clear objective. We use a design thinking
   approach, where we find a real person in the world who
   is experiencing a real problem. Then, our learners go to
   work solving that real problem.
2. Curate resources. Different from usual pre-packaged curriculum, the educator provides learners with suggested
   resources to explore as they set about addressing the
   problem through their learning project.

3. Provide exemplars. What does world-class work in this field look like? Show learners examples of high-quality work that they can learn from and compare their own work against.

4. Bring in experts. Instead of seeing the teacher as the content expert, have the teacher facilitate connections to actual industry experts that can provide honest feedback to learners on the iterations of their work.

5. Embrace iteration. Give learners time to work through a design process that provides numerous feedback loops and grants them opportunities to revise and improve their work.

6. Showcase mastery. Make the learning public. Have learners exhibit their learning in a showcase. Invite experts to evaluate their work. Invite the user (the real person with the real problem).

7. Reflect and assess. Set aside ample time for learners to reflect on how they showed up for the project. Give them access to the feedback from the experts and the users. Facilitate "meaning-making" with students so that they can clearly understand the feedback. Provide reflection prompts that allow them to assess the strengths and areas of improvement in their projects.

Examples:
Northern Cass School District uses an approach called "Studios," where learners can create their own projects that replace one or multiple high school courses. Crossroads College Preparatory School has a 5th Day Program, where learners tackle transdisciplinary projects that arise from problems of practice within the community.

Reflection Prompts
System Element: Curriculum, Pedagogy, and Assessment

Biggest Ripple Effect: Community Practices and School Culture (celebrating learning from failure and reflection); Communications (what gets emphasized in external communications)

What is it and Why:
Going back to the theme of this chapter, "Focusing on the Whole Child," reflection prompts provide a great opportunity for students to deeply consider who they are, what they're interested in, what struggles they're experiencing, and their goals moving forward. Reflection prompts can live at any place in the schedule, in any learning experience, and should be used often to prompt meta-cognitive thinking. Here are some ideas for how to use them:

How to do it:
1. Build in reflection to *each* and *every* learning experience. Make it a deliverable that each student is on the hook for. There are a lot of examples and resources out there you can utilize. It could be as simple as having students complete the phrase: "I used to think...but now I think." It could be an opportunity to jot down a brief list of things they learned and a few questions they still have. It could be a simple self-survey where they assess their own engagement/work. Make reflection a rhythm, so much so that every learning experience *feels* incomplete without it.
2. Make "big picture" reflections a key part of being at the school. Have learners create their own progress reports and after-action reviews, highlighting their goals, their progress on their goals, their strengths, weaknesses, and plans to grow.
3. Provide ample avenues of feedback and time for learners to reflect. At The Forest School, feedback comes from peers, external experts, and educators. Learners then have

time in the schedule to wrestle with the feedback, make meaning of it, and process the feedback through a written reflection.

Belonging Surveys

System Element: Community Practices and School Culture

Biggest Ripple Effect: Continuous Improvement Mechanisms (what to do with the results); Tech and Tech Infrastructure (how to administer the surveys)

What it is and Why:
How confident are you as a leader that each and every student feels a deep sense of belonging at school? An easy way to find out is to ask them! At The Forest School, we created anonymous surveys where students can rate their own feelings of belonging, their closeness to their peers and educators, and identify when and how they may feel othered or ostracized. This gives us data to reflect on ourselves and take back to the learners so that we can brainstorm together how to do better.

How to do it:
1. Create a simple anonymous survey.
2. Keep it simple. Here are some example questions:
    1. On a scale from 1 to 10, I feel like I can be my true self here.
    2. On a scale from 1 to 10, I feel loved and welcomed by my peers.
    3. On a scale from 1 to 10, I feel like features of my identity (race, religion, culture, etc.) are welcome in the classroom.
    4. One thing the class can do to be more inclusive is…
3. Learn from the data! Reflect on it with your leadership team. What do you notice? What does it make you think?

4. Take it back to the learners. Have the class reflect on the data. Make sense of it together. Co-create ideas on how to make the class *even more* welcoming and inclusive.

Conclusion

Children are beautifully complex. Often, the systems of accountability and compliance of traditional schools minimize that complexity. Students became a GPA, a data point of test scores. What if, instead, we saw them as people who have real thoughts, plans, and ideas? What if school was a place where they were encouraged to be their true, authentic selves? Where they were celebrated for who they are? Where they practiced the messy work of learning to live together with other people across lines of difference? What would these schools look and feel like? More importantly, what kind of graduates would they send out into the world?

This playbook is incomplete, but it's a starting point. Hopefully, these techniques can kickstart your own thinking about the kind of leader you want to be, the kind of school you want to lead, the kind of team you want to assemble, and the kinds of experiences you want your students to have. It's hard work. It's messy work. But it's important work.

The rest of the chapters will equip you with even more techniques to cultivate a learner-led, character-forging environment where every student feels seen, celebrated, and supported to be the very best versions of themselves.

References

Craft, S. (2023, October 30). *Average GPA in high school 2024 and past years - ThinkImpact.* ThinkImpact.com. https://www.thinkimpact. com/average-gpa-in-high-school/

Mastery Transcript Consortium. (2024, May 15). *Welcome to Mastery Transcript Consortium (MTC)*. Mastery Transcript Consortium (MTC) https://mastery.org/

Posner, R. (2009). *Lives of Passion, Schools of Hope*. Sentient Publications.

UNESCO (1997). Educating for a Sustainable Future: A Transdisciplinary Vision for Concerted Action. https://unesdoc.unesco.org/ark:/48223/pf0000110686

Valor – powered by Compass | Develop Students. Build Communities. (2022, July 1). Valor Compass. http://www.poweredbycompass.org/

4

Promoting Student and Educator Choice

At the heart of self-directed learning is the idea of choice. If I am leading my own learning, then I have meaningful choices to make. These choices may involve what I am working on, when I'm working on it, what resources I'm pulling from, how I'm being evaluated, who I'm working with, etc. This will perhaps be the hardest chapter for many school leaders and educators. Many of us went to schools where we had little say in the rules or curriculum. Our own teaching and administrative experience, likewise, was probably lacking in meaningful choices. All the training we've received is probably more about control and management than letting go of those things and transferring power to children. This is where the rubber meets the road when talking about self-directed learning. At the end of the day, do we really believe that learners can lead their own learning?

In this chapter, we'll outline techniques that you can use to cultivate choice both with your teams and with the learners at your

DOI: 10.4324/9781003489894-4

school. Increasingly, schools have become places where not only learner choice is stifled, but teacher choice as well. As a school leader, how might you lean into the choices of your team? How might they feel even more empowered to make meaningful choices in their work? Have you built a culture where everyone feels valued? Do your team members have space to bring their own ideas, plans, and dreams into their work? What are the constraints, the intentionally created guardrails, that guide their choices? How can choice be maximized for students in a classroom context where standards are expected or the curriculum is more rigid?

A Story

In 2019, we received this email from one of our learners at The Forest School:

> I am sending this email because I would like to talk to you about a situation that I have been running into with Khan Academy. Unfortunately over the past couple of months I have realized that I have not been learning as much math as I should be. I feel like I am not learning anything from Khan Academy, and these past couple of months I have been wasting my time on a platform that I don't understand. Anyway, I think I have a solution to this problem. To put together a system that works for my learning type. I have some ideas and a proposal that I would like to get your thoughts on. Do you have time in the next couple of days to meet with me to discuss more?

You can imagine how excited we were! A learner took it upon themselves to identify a struggle, create a proposal for a solution, and reach out to us to discuss it. This learner was in 7th grade at the time, but here she was, advocating for herself and her desire to *choose* a math program that worked for her. As it turns out, she actually craved a textbook and worksheets. Trying to watch videos and work on an e-learning platform was more frustrating to her than following a textbook. So, we worked with her to get physical materials and she used those to build her math knowledge.

Think about how you (whether you're a classroom teacher or school/district-level leader) can create space for learners to have meaningful choices in their education. For this student, that didn't necessitate any bending of standards or pacing: just a different medium for practice. But that small change made all the difference to her.

Techniques

Guardrails for Innovation

System Element: Vision

Biggest Ripple Effect: Curriculum, Pedagogy, and Assessment

What it is and Why:
Good leaders want to equip their teams to try new things, take risks, and innovate in their classrooms. Without a cohesive structure, though, this freedom to create may impede the work of the school by not being mission/vision aligned, by not cultivating the outcomes listed in the Portrait of a Graduate, or by causing miscommunication among educators, learners, parents/caregivers, and other stakeholders. It's important, then, for leaders to clearly articulate the guardrails, the design constraints for planning challenges, making schedules, organizing classroom furniture and wall postings, communicating with learners and parents, and knowing how, when, and where educators can test new ideas.

How to do it:

1. Gather all of your "North Star" documents, including mission/vision statements, the Portrait of a Graduate, and design principles.
2. List out all of the signature learning experiences that students encounter at your school. These are discrete, time-bound learning opportunities that are intentionally designed to cultivate specific learner outcomes (think about the blocks in your schedule).
3. For each signature learning experience, what *must* be true about it, each and every time? List those out.
4. Create your Guardrails for Innovation. Consider assembling a simple slide deck. The first slides reiterate the "North Star" documents (from Step 1). The rest of the slides walk through each signature learning experience, highlighting the *must-haves* for each one and giving clarity for when and where educators can experiment.
5. Coach your team on the Guardrails for Innovation and revisit them often!

A Continuum of Teacher-Centered/Student-Centered Education

System Element: Vision

Biggest Ripple Effect: Curriculum, Pedagogy, and Assessment; Community Practices and School Culture; Communication

What it is and why:

Frederick County Public Schools in Virginia have developed an excellent teacher resource that highlights the continuum that exists between teacher-directed and student-directed learning (see Figure 4.1). This framework was created by teachers and for teachers to promote student choice within the constraints of public education. They call the framework "Inspire: The Continuum of Teaching and Learning" and have identified spectra that exist for students to direct their design, facilitation, and reflection of their own learning.

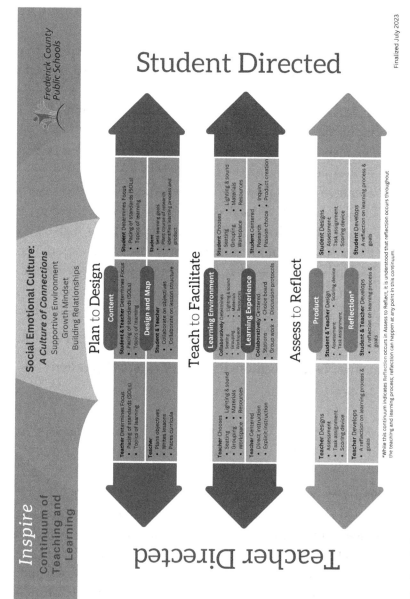

FIGURE 4.1 Frederick County Public Schools Continuum of Teaching and Learning.

How to do it:

Rather than a step-by-step "how to," this is an invitation to reflect on the continuum above. The process of creating this framework was years long, with many rounds of feedback and revision from teachers and school/district leadership. The teachers that served as the architects of the framework started by asking teachers two simple questions:

- ◆ What's in your locus of control?
- ◆ What's not in your locus of control?

Those conversations were the starting place in developing the continuum. They designed the continuum as a tool to free teachers to increase student agency *if they so wished*. The continuum isn't prescriptive, nor is it used as an evaluation tool in teacher assessment. Teachers could choose to stay on the "teacher-centered" side of the continuum. Or, if they wanted, they had clear steps to push toward a more student-centered classroom. So, as a school leader, reflect on how you could utilize a tool like this with your leadership team. How would you go about creating your own? What sort of buy-in would you need to get from your leadership team, teachers, parents/caregivers, and students? The act alone of creating a framework like this would prove immensely helpful in moving your school towards learner agency.

Designing Signature Learning Experiences

System Element: Curriculum, Pedagogy, and Assessment

Biggest Ripple Effect: Schedules and Routines; Roles

What it is and Why:

We mentioned signature learning experiences in an earlier technique. Again, these are discrete, time-bound, learning opportunities that are intentionally designed to cultivate specific learner outcomes. Designing choice-filled signature learning experiences is one of the single most effective tools an educator has in their toolbox for promoting agency. Think about the blocks in your schedule. Consider each and every activity your students move between throughout the day. Each of those is an intentionally designed experience. Designing signature learning experiences to promote choice is not a perfect science. We'll provide some ideas to get started.

How to do it:

1. Start by creating your Guardrails for Innovation (see previous technique). This will give you and your team the design constraints to build engaging signature learning experiences.
2. With your Portrait of a Graduate in mind, create signature learning experiences that will give each student practice at the outcomes you are seeking to cultivate:
   1. Name the target outcome of the experience.
   2. Name how the target outcome will be measured/ assessed.
   3. Create the deliverables. Strong signature learning experiences will have deliverables in the following categories:
      1. Individual (Public): These are deliverables that learners "make public" by showcasing to an external audience (peers, experts, parents/caregivers, and other community members).
      2. Individual (Private): There are deliverables related to the project, but not intended for a public audience. These could be drafts, notes, or prototypes.
      3. Group (Public): This is the "public-facing" portion of a collaborative project, shown to an external audience (peers, experts, parents/caregivers, and other community members).

4. Group (Private): There are deliverables related to the project, but not intended for a public audience. These could be drafts, notes, or prototypes.

4. Consider the user experience. Put yourself in the shoes of an outside observer. Complete the sentence: "If I visited, I would see..." Imagine feedback from stakeholders. Complete the sentences: "If asked, learners would say...parents would say...my teammates would say..."

3. With each signature learning experience, include the following modalities (in varying order):

1. Discuss: Learners have time to "sense-make" together. *Tips to cultivate student choice*: empower learners to create the Rules of Engagement for discussions; have learners lead discussions; provide forced-choice options ("Would you (A) or (B)?"); solicit feedback from learners on the discussion and record what questions they'd like to explore further.

2. Explore: Learners utilize curated resources to further their own understanding, as well as encounter world-class examples of work in this field. *Tips to cultivate student choice*: guide learners to find, vet, and utilize their own resources; empower learners to follow their natural curiosity; provide world-class examples and industry-specific rubrics for learners to compare their work to.

3. Make: Learners are on the hook to create something as they engage with the learning experience. *Tips to cultivate student choice*: give learners options to choose from in terms of deliverable; let learners choose to work individually or in groups; provide a rotating menu of modalities.

4. Share: There is dedicated time for learners to share their work (with peers, educators, and/or experts). *Tips to cultivate student choice*: Provide a menu of options learners can choose from in presenting their work.

5. Evaluate: There is a way for learners to receive evaluation/feedback on their work (through self-reflection, peer review, educator feedback, or expert evaluation). *Tips to cultivate student choice*: empower learners to choose how their work is assessed.

6. Reflect: Learners are given prompts and time to metacognitively reflect on their learning experience. *Tips to cultivate student choice*: provide a menu of reflection prompts for learners to engage with.

7. Submit: Each learner is expected to "turn in" a specific deliverable. *Tips to cultivate student choice*: provide options for deliverables and diversify modalities.

4. Give educators flexibility. Using the Guardrails for Innovation and the above modalities, educators become experts at designing for deep learning. Where do signature learning experiences live on the schedule? How much time are learners given for each one? How often do they encounter them? These can be freedoms given to educators, as long as each learner is getting deliberate practice at each and every outcome in your Portrait of a Graduate.

Choice-Filled Learning Plans

System Element: Curriculum, Assessment, and Pedagogy

Biggest Ripple Effect: Roles (training teachers to manage the quality of learning through multiple channels)

The What and the Why:

We mentioned Customized Learning Plans in the last chapter, but it bears repeating here as we discuss how to boost student choice. What if each learner had a say in what they were learning (i.e., outcomes) and the pathway they took to learn it (i.e., curriculum)? At many learner-led schools, each learner not only *can* but is *strongly encouraged* to modify their learning plan. Learners, in concert with caregivers and educators, create their own units of study, identify the resources they use, the milestones they'll meet, and determine how they will demonstrate mastery.

How to do it:

1. Using your Portrait of a Graduate, identify all the *required* skills, mindsets, and knowledge all of your learners are on the hook for.
2. Guide learners to create a learning plan that encompasses all the required competencies *but leaves room for self-selected courses.*
3. Create a protocol for learners to add, subtract, or change their learning plans. At The Forest School, we provide learners with a checklist to consider as they create a new course. New courses need to be signed off on by educators and caregivers. (Sometimes this can be an earned privilege: new learners that show that they can meet their learning goals are given greater and greater autonomy on their learning plans).
4. Create a school that has "porous walls." Provide lots of opportunities for learners to hear about, try out, and engage a wide range of interests that they can pursue *where they are* by tapping the expertise of the community.
5. Celebrate learners that pursue their interests!

Customized Learning Targets

System Element: Curriculum, Pedagogy, and Assessment

Biggest Ripple Effect: Roles

What it is and Why:
Clayton Moon, a history and sociology teacher in Pike County, Georgia, developed a student-directed approach in his high school classes. Every period, he provides students the material

they are supposed to cover that day in regards to the district pacing guide. Each student explores the material and decides on their own "learning target," a high-interest concept they want to know more about. Each learner researches their learning target, then they take turns teaching each other. Clayton records all the learning targets identified by learners and keeps them on the board. Over the course of a unit, those learning targets become the backbone of their assessments. "When it comes time for the final," he said, "I tell them they already know the questions. They came up with them."

How to do it:

1. When delivering a lesson, allow students to search the materials (textbooks, videos, articles, etc.) and choose their own learning targets.
2. Give students time to do a deep dive on their learning targets, synthesize their knowledge, and create notes to teach others.
3. Facilitate a "share" time (1-on-1 or small groups) for students to teach each other about their learning targets.
4. Record and visually present the learning targets that students choose for themselves. Clayton guides his students to look at all of the learning targets and identify themes and categories. Consider using these in your assessments.

Flexible Seating

System Element: Facilities

Biggest Ripple Effect: Budget, Operations and Logistics (furniture); Roles (training staff in how to deploy)

What it is and Why:
This chapter is all about choice. Seating is an easy place to hand off choice to learners and is usually a factor of the learning design

that is well within the control of the educator. So, where are learners working? We'll do a deep dive into the learning environment in Chapter 11, addressing elements like furniture, lighting, and wall hangings. Here, let's zero in on the simple choice of seating. As a school leader, how can you empower your team to open up simple choices like seating for learners?

How to do it:

1. Design flexible learning environments that can facilitate multiple modalities in learning. In the "Designing Signature Learning Experiences" technique we highlighted earlier, we identified seven modalities: discuss, explore, make, share, evaluate, submit, and reflect. The seating options in the classroom should be able to accommodate all of those modalities. How can learners easily transition between discussion, exploration, and making? The seating should be able to shift from individual to collaborative work.

2. Let learners choose where to work. A common objection we hear is "But what if learners are distracting themselves and others?" Here are some ideas to address this question:

   1. Make seating choice an earned freedom. At many self-directed schools, especially with our younger learners, the freedom to choose where you work is "unlocked" as students display responsibility. Maybe learners who are meeting their goals can choose their seats?

   2. Embrace natural consequences. Maybe all students start with the freedom to choose their seating, but this freedom can be temporarily lost if they are causing distractions in the classroom.

   3. Play the long game. Some students may indeed distract themselves and others by their seating choices.

This can actually be a really rich learning experience. Empower students to give each other regular feedback on how the behavior of their peers impacts the class. Also, have regular check-ins with learners to stay abreast of their progress on their learning goals. If a learner is consistently behind on their goals and if they're also receiving regular feedback from their peers about disruptive behavior, then that learner can *act* on the feedback they're receiving. Learning self-regulation skills is vital for a young person. Having early and consistent practice (in a low-risk environment) of having to monitor and adjust their focused attention builds the muscles of learners to direct their own learning.

Something to consider:
When learners choose their seating, they often opt to congregate with peers with similar identities and backgrounds (along lines of race, gender, culture, language, etc.). Beverly Tatum's book *Why Are All the Black Kids Sitting Together in the Cafeteria? And Other Conversations about Race* (Tatum 2003) is a great resource on this dynamic. To build a multicultural, diverse-by-design environment, you will need to consider how to allow learners freedom to self-select into groups *and* how you can encourage them to build relationships across lines of difference. An important role of the educator is to facilitate connections. Use team-building activities to give learners structured practice in getting to know all of their peers, not just those they select to be around.

Rules, Norms, and Consequences

System Element: Community Practices and School Culture

Biggest Ripple Effect: Vision; Communication; and Roles

What it is and Why:

Most students spend their days following rules that some-one else made. They had no voice in the rules. They didn't get to speak to the consequences. They didn't get to shape the "norms" that govern their space. What if, instead, learners put their fingerprints all over the rules, norms, and consequences that they have to abide by? Rather than adult-given rules and consequences, what if they got to experience the natural con-sequences of their choices immediately? In our experience, two important things happen: (1) the systems that learners create are *better* than the systems adults create, and (2) there are far fewer behavior issues when learners themselves are governing their space. We'll do a deep dive on this in Chapter 7, but here are some tips for getting started.

How to do it:

1. Through onboarding and professional development, make sure your educators are 100% aware of and bought into the mission, vision, and design principles of the school and have a thorough knowledge of your Guardrails for Innovation.

2. Center safety, respect, and responsibility. Giving students the freedom to create the rules doesn't mean we (as caring adults) don't have the responsibility to ensure each learn-er's safety (physical and emotional) as well as enforce the non-negotiable that everyone will be respected at all times.

3. Dedicate the early weeks of the school year to self-gover-nance. Before you dive into academics, guide learners through a supportive process of designing their own environment. This can easily be scaffolded. One idea is to provide a long list of "suggested" rules and have students choose which ones they want to experiment with.

4. Provide world-class input and feedback. Invite local civic leaders (city council, mayors, etc.), business leaders, contract experts, and professional negotiators to give students feedback on the early drafts of their governance structures.

5. Memorialize the agreed-upon rules in a "Contract." After weeks of iteration, our classes agree upon the rules that will govern their spaces by creating a Contract of Promises. We have a public moment where the learners sign their names to this contact and agree to be held accountable to it.

6. Make the Contract visible. Post it on a wall in the classroom. Refer to it daily.

7. Hold up a mirror. When the class isn't living into the promises they made to each other, simply call out the behavior and refer to the contract. Bring them into the decision-making process. Ask, "What should we do, change our Contract or change our behavior?" Students want to operate in a well-structured, well-governed space. Give them opportunities to address their shortcomings in self-governance and make improvements as a community.

Schedules

System Elements: Schedules and Routines

Biggest Ripple Effect: Roles (staff deployment); Facilities (space design and organization)

What it is and Why:
We all have constraints on our time. A school schedule is another place to open up choice for educators and students. How much of their day is dictated by school leadership or curriculum? What if, instead, educators had agency over their daily schedules? And,

what if, within those schedules, students were also able to make key decisions about how they spend their time?

Constraints:

We know, we know—schedules are some of the biggest constraints teachers experience. Often when it comes to education innovation, educators are expected to put *more* things into an already packed schedule. Our encouragement is to find windows where you could do *less*. Where in your daily/weekly schedules can you give students meaningful choice in what they're working on? Here are some ideas:

♦ Create a choice-based block. Some schools have a study hall or "Genius Hour" block where students can choose what they want to explore. Crossroads College Preparatory Academy in St. Louis, Missouri has a "5th Day" program, where one day of the week is dedicated to guiding students to design and explore a project aligned with their own interests and passions. When learners have a block of time that is their own, they build the skills of time management, self-pacing, and project mapping (the ability to break down a long-term project into smaller deliverables).

♦ In a subject-oriented course, offer a "menu" for students to choose from. For example, in a Language Arts class, learners could choose to read, write, or participate in a critique circle where they give each other feedback on a piece of writing.

♦ Have learners give feedback on the schedule. One idea is to have them vote on how they want to spend a course block ("Would you rather do (option a), (option b), or (option c)?"). This is a small but effective way to increase democratic engagement with learners. The more say they have over the schedule, the more learners will be engaged with the work.

How school leaders can help:

1. Give educators more freedom to draw up their daily and weekly schedules, choosing which signature learning experiences to explore.

2. Through coaching and feedback, help educators course correct when needed. One school we worked with realized that their learners weren't getting enough writing practice throughout the week. They were able to pivot and create more writing-centered deliverables, timely feedback from experts, and opportunities for learners to share their work publicly.

3. Resist adding *more* to the schedules of educators and students. Research has shown that the concept of "slack"—having flexibility in scheduled routines—decreases teacher burnout and increases learner motivation (Raab, 2017).

Conclusion

In this chapter, we've highlighted how educators and learners alike can have greater freedom in the classroom. Educators (following the Guardrails for Innovation created by the leadership team) have freedom to design their learning experiences and create their schedules. Learners have freedom to choose the content they are exploring, the rules that govern their space, and where they're working, and who they're working with. There will be constraints in any learning environment. The balancing act for forward-thinking school leaders and educators is working within those constraints to maximize the meaningful choices young people can make. As students and educators experience greater degrees of freedom in their work, they more eagerly and earnestly co-create a flourishing learning environment.

References

Raab, E. (2017). *Why school? A systems perspective on creating schooling for flourishing individuals and a thriving democratic society* [PhD thesis]. Doctoral Thesis Stanford University. https://www.academia.edu/35043849/Why_School_A_Systems_Perspective_on_Creating_Schooling_for_Flourishing_Individuals_and_a_Thriving_Democratic_Society

Tatum, B. (2003). *Why Are All the Black Kids Sitting Together in the Cafeteria? And Other Conversations About Race*. Basic Books.

5

Facilitating Daily Student Goal Setting

A foundation of self-directed learning is that learners have choice and agency to make meaningful progress on *their* own goals and plans. Much of leading traditional school environments involves motivating students to tackle pre-decided standards and curriculum and tracking their progress. It takes a major mindset shift, then, to pivot from imposing curriculum and pacing on students and instead empowering them to set goals that are aligned with their own interests *and also* connected to the school's Portrait of a Graduate.

It might be helpful to think about how you, as an adult, go about learning how to do something new. It could be a hobby (playing guitar, painting), it could be a professional skill (coding, graphic design), it could be for personal growth (a new language, habit, or discipline), or it could be tied to a career pathway (continuing education). In all of those cases, the pathway would be similar. You start by defining the desired outcome. What do you want to be true about learning this new thing? Then you break the thing into its fundamental parts and create your own scope and

DOI: 10.4324/9781003489894-5

sequence. What do you need to learn first? What comes next? Then set deadlines. By *when* do you need to learn x so that you can go onto y? What will hold you accountable in this learning endeavor?

That whole process, from defining the outcome to plotting the first step, is the heart of goal setting. In later chapters we will go in detail about what happens next, like identifying relevant resources and getting actionable feedback, but for now, let's zero in on the act of goal setting. How can you as a school leader build the muscles of your team and your learners to successfully set and meet ambitious goals?

A Story

An experimental public school, The Center for Self-Directed Learning, opened in 1972 in a Chicago suburb. "The Center," as it was known, was a school-within-a-school, housed in New Trier East High School. The founding staff of the school were deeply influenced by Carl Roger's (1969) *Freedom to Learn*, a text that made strong arguments for self-directed learning (SDL) and inspired researchers and practitioners to more deeply explore SDL in the subsequent decades. The Center was established as an alternative school within an already established high school. As Bellanco, Paul, and Paul (2014) observed: "Unlike today, when the term 'alternative' refers to a place to assign especially troublesome special needs students, this experimental program embraced all students who wanted to enter" (p. 2). As far as curriculum went, students at the center did have to complete certain state-required courses, but it was up to the student and their faculty advisor as to how to complete the course. In general, a student of The Center had to prove they had mastered SDL in order to graduate. To do this, there was a seven-step process:

> Students would have to show their proficiencies to make an authentic goal of high personal importance, find resources (wherever or whatever those may be in a range

of learning experiences from one course in the parent school per semester to internships, field studies, small group investigations, a research study, or travel to Italy), identify a facilitator/evaluator (wherever or whomever had the expertise from The Center, the parent school, community college or university faculty member, practicing artists, parents, businesspersons, medical researchers, inventors, etc.), follow a self-planned weekly schedule, produce evidence of learning, assess that learning with criteria, and show how the specific learning contributed to college preparation, life, and/or career goals which the students were also forming at the same time.

(p. 4)

Notice the sequence in the seven-step process. The first step was setting a personal, relevant, authentic goal. To cultivate self-directed learners, it's important that you as a school leader and educator first guide students to become great goal-setters. The techniques below are a starting place.

Techniques

Educator Competencies and Professional Growth Tracker
System Element: Roles

Biggest Ripple Effect: Onboarding; Communications; Vision

What it is and Why:
In earlier chapters, we emphasized the significance of redefining the educator's role and establishing comprehensive onboarding procedures to ensure their success in a learner-led environment. Equally crucial is implementing a thoughtful professional growth process that enables educators to establish their own goals, reflect on their progress, and make necessary adjustments when required.

How to do it:

1. Clearly define the roles and responsibilities of educators in your school.
2. Guide your team to evaluate their strengths and areas of growth against the roles and responsibilities you have outlined.
3. Have your team set ambitious but realistic goals for their professional development.
4. Create multiple feedback loops for your team. We guide our educators through a comprehensive self-reflection, have them give feedback to their teammates, and provide each of them actionable feedback from the leadership team.
5. After reflecting on the feedback, each team member sets new goals and discusses those goals with the leadership team.
6. Celebrate wins! Publicly acknowledge your teammates when they set and meet challenging goals.

SMART and WOOP Goals

What it is and Why:

Goal setting is a practiced habit. With all habits, it takes structure, practice, and discipline to build over time. Many of us don't know where to start when it comes to setting meaningful goals in our work. Here are two protocols you can use yourself, practice with your team, and handoff to learners.

SMART Goals:

This protocol is common in the world of work. SMART is an acronym for:

◆ Specific: Are your goals focused enough? Set a goal for one task at a time.

♦ Measurable: Can you track progress on your goal? Is there some sort of unit (time, percentage, etc.) that you can measure?

♦ Achievable: Is this goal *doable*? Is it something you can reasonably accomplish?

♦ Relevant: Is this goal relevant to your larger learning plan? Will meeting this goal help you make progress on your big picture goals?

♦ Time-bound: Does this goal have a reasonable time horizon (be it minutes, hours, days, or weeks)? Setting time-bound goals allows you to reflect on your progress and pivot as needed.

WOOP Goals:

Another goal-setting protocol, WOOP goals allow you to anticipate potential obstacles and make a plan for overcoming them. WOOP stands for:

♦ Wish: What is it you're wanting to accomplish? Why is it important?

♦ Outcome: What will happen if you accomplish this goal? How will it help you? What will happen if you fail to accomplish this goal?

♦ Obstacles: What are the barriers in your way? What will impede your ability to meet this goal?

♦ Plan: What's your plan to overcome the obstacles and mitigate barriers?

How to do it:

1. Make goal setting a key part of the culture of your school. As a leader, make your own goals public to your team. Do they know what your goals are? Do they see your reflection process? Do you make them aware of pivots you make along the way?

2. Make goal setting an important part of professional growth. At The Forest School, our team makes professional

goals together, reflects on them throughout the year, and pivots when necessary.

3. Give learners protocols to use (like SMART or WOOP goals).

4. Make wall postings. Put resources on a poster that can be easily referenced.

5. Build it into the schedule. Have dedicated time for students to set their goals. (We'll look at this more in-depth below).

6. Create an accountability system. Pair learners up into goal-setting partners. (We'll look at this more in-depth below). Or have a public board for learners to post their goals. Every added layer of accountability helps learners stay mindful of their goals.

7. Give parents language to use. (We'll look at this more in-depth below). We equip our parents to at least ask two questions every week. On Monday morning, we expect parents to ask learners about their larger learning goals for that week. And on Friday afternoon, we expect them to ask their learners how they progressed on their goals.

Goal-Setting Partners

System Element: Community Practices and School Culture

Biggest Ripple Effect: Schedules and Routines; Roles

What it is and Why

We're more likely to stick to our goals if we make them known to other people. A "buddy system" of goal setting allows learners to connect with a peer to set goals together, give each other feedback on goals, and revisit progress on goals. Goal Setting Partners (called Accountability Buddies at Khan Lab School and Running Partners at Acton Academy) are pairs of learners who work together daily to set goals and monitor progress. Partners are randomly chosen by educators, usually at the start of each session. Educators choose partners so learners get to experience as many people in their classroom as possible, not just their friends.

Every day, usually in the morning, partners set daily goals together. They encourage each other and hold each other accountable. They provide emotional support, picking each other up when they're down. For Goal Setting Partners to really work, learners have to take ownership of the dynamic between them, put in the effort, and make the most of their time together. They have to initiate daily meetings to set goals and check in. They have to be open to listening to feedback. Partners often end up being the first-place learners go for advice, feedback, or personal support throughout the year.

How to do it:

1. This is only going to be effective if you've made goal setting a key part of the learning culture. If it's not, then this is just going to be a box that learners check instead of an experience they engage with.

2. Equip your educators with tips and techniques for facilitating Goal Setting Partners. This can include:
   1. Protocols like SMART and WOOP Goals.
   2. A template that learners complete.
   3. Guiding questions to ask students as they set their goals.

3. Give educators flexibility to facilitate peer goal setting in a way that best meets the needs of the class.

4. Educators need to be intentional with groupings. Why is one learner paired with another? Maybe they have similar interests and can build upon them. Maybe they are very different in their interests and personalities and can challenge each other to grow. Maybe they rarely speak to each other and pairing them is a point of connection. Maybe one learner is an expert goal setter and the other

is still struggling to build the muscles. It doesn't matter what the reason is, but there should be one.

5. Be consistent but remain flexible. For goal setting to become a habit, there does need to be consistency in a system like Goal Setting Partners. However, there is a lot of room to create and pivot. Do partners stay the same, or change every week or month? Does one pair of partners group up with other pairs to form a Goal Setting Squad? Do the guiding questions/templates change over time?

6. Build-in a feedback loop. Learners should be able to give their partners feedback on how they showed up. This should be educator-facilitated and simple, maybe as basic as three questions:

   1. On a scale from 1 to 10, how well did your partner aid you in setting and meeting your goals?
   2. What is one thing your partner did that was helpful to you as you set your goals?
   3. What is one thing your partner can improve on to be even better at helping you set goals and holding you accountable?

The role of the learner is to:

1. Meet with their partner every morning to set goals and review their progress.
   1. Encourage learners to update their partners on what their goals are, what they've accomplished, and what challenges they're facing.
   2. Provide prompt questions for them to discuss like: "What do you plan to do today?" "What have you accomplished?" "What are you challenged by?"
2. Offer feedback and encouragement to one another.
   1. Partners develop the skills to be able to ask each other, "Why are you doing that? Can you tell me why

these are your goals? Do you think you could reach for something more challenging?" Encourage learners to hold each other to high standards.

2. Encourage learners to discuss the challenges they're facing. Goal Setting Partners can help learners troubleshoot and find solutions, imagine possibilities they hadn't seen before, and examine needs and resources.

3. Self-reflect on the feedback they receive.
    1. Be open to what they have to say, take the time to look over their challenges for the week and give them constructive feedback.

4. Offer practical help.
    1. Encourage learners to share practical needs with one another. Whether they need someone to edit an essay, help with research for a project, or emotional support during a tough time, Goal Setting Partners are there to lend a hand and lift each other up.

What you need:

♦ A strategy for pairing learners, or a hat to pull names from if you prefer a random selection.

♦ Time to share the idea of Goal Setting Partners with learners, answer questions, and provide guidance for how they can get the most out of their time together.

♦ Time to check in with learners to see how their Goal Setting Partner experience is going.

Pro Tip:

This technique can be adapted into small groups of peers, which can be especially helpful for younger learners. The concept is the same, but instead four or more learners are assigned to work together. This provides more support and diversity for learners who are still developing the skills needed to set realistic goals and offer valuable feedback.

Scheduled Goal Setting

System Element: Community Practices and School Culture

Biggest Ripple Effect: Schedules and Routines; Roles

What it is and Why:

This chapter has already covered numerous techniques to facilitate goal setting. We've discussed that setting goals is a habit, a muscle that must be strengthened over time. It's important that students get regular, consistent practice at setting their goals. Class schedules are already bursting at the seams with all of the amazing opportunities we want learners to experience. Where does goal setting fit in? Here are some ideas.

How to do it:

1. Prioritize goal setting. *Especially* in the early days and weeks of the school year, provide learners with regular, scaffolded practice at setting their goals.
2. Put it on the daily schedule. This can be a short session (10–15 minutes) for learners to get with their Partner and discuss their goals for that day.
3. Add in daily reflection. Have learners set goals in the morning, then revisit their goals in the afternoon. How did they do? Guide them to reflect on their progress. Here are some prompts you can use:
    1. If a learner met their goals…
        1. What did you do today to help you achieve your goals?
        2. Did meeting your goals today help you stay on track with your weekly, monthly, and yearly goals?
        3. Do you think you need to set more ambitious goals tomorrow?
        4. Did your partner meet their goals? How did you support them?

2. If a learner didn't meet their goals…
    1. Were your goals too ambitious? Do you need to set more reasonable goals tomorrow?
    2. Were you too distracted? Do you need to sit somewhere else tomorrow? Do you have strategies for getting into flow (noise-canceling headphones, putting your phone away, etc.)?
    3. Does your partner know you struggled to meet your goals? Have you asked them for help/advice?
    4. Did your partner meet their goals? How did you support them?
4. Add in larger goal-setting sessions at the beginning of the week or the beginning of a unit. This allows learners to "calibrate" their daily goal setting to meet their longer-term goals.

An Example

Synergy, in the Mineola School District in New York, begins their day with students setting goals with a learning coach. The goals are broadcast on a screen for clarity, alignment, and accountability. After a work session, learners have a "check out" with their learning coach where they reflect on the progress they've made. If learners are consistently missing their goals, coaches work with teachers to assign direct instruction and small group classwork.

Mid-Action & After Action Reviews

System Element: Assessment

Biggest Ripple Effect: Communications (reporting out); Roles (training to facilitate reflection)

What is it and Why:

We've said it before in this book: reflection is the key to deep learning. If a student is periodically taking stock of their progress, evaluating their learning, and adjusting their short-term goals in alignment with their long-term goals, then they're going to struggle to lead their own education. After Action Reviews (AARs) originated in the military. After a mission, personnel would walk through a process to determine if the mission was a success and what tweaks they need to make next time. This practice seeped into the business world, with companies doing AARs after events and project launches. We think it's a helpful practice in education as well.

How to do it:

1. Think about doing two thorough "reviews" each year, one at the midpoint of the school year (we call these Mid-Action Reviews, or MARs) and then the AAR at the end of the school year.
2. The backbone of an AAR (as used in the military and business worlds) is four questions:
    1. What did you set out to do?
    2. What actually happened?
    3. Is there a difference between what you set out to do and what happened?
    4. What should you do differently next time?
3. Obviously, those questions should be in language that is developmentally appropriate to the age group you're working with.
4. Weave in your Portrait of a Graduate and the learner's customized plan. We prompt learners to reflect on their progress on all categories, provide examples of their best work, highlight key struggles/frustrations, and set goals for moving forward.

5. Guide learners to complete their MARs/AARs. This will need to be scaffolded. Put time into the schedule. This should be a low-anxiety, low-lift process for all parties.

6. Create a time for learners to share their MARs/AARs with their parents/caregivers and Dream Teams. This can be in school (in a conference setting) or out of school (over a meal, for example). Incentivize completion of this process.

Educator–Learner Goal-Setting Check-Ins

System Element: Community Practices and School Culture

Biggest Ripple Effect: Pedagogy (teachers as guides), Schedules and Routines (to make time for this), Roles (for educators to provide one-on-one guidance and coaching; staff have to be deployed in creative ways to make this happen), and Facilities (making space for it).

What is it and Why:
You'll notice that the technique of Check-ins is listed in multiple chapters in this book. This is a vital practice for educators to build and maintain relationships with their students, gain insight into their learning progress, and support them going forward. Here, we'll highlight how Check-ins are an important part of the goal-setting process.

How to do it:
1. Educators need to schedule time to have one-on-one meetings with their learners. The cadence of these Check-ins will depend on class size and educator capacity.

2. Check-ins are learner-led, but educators still need a template with questions to ask. We've found success in creating Google Docs with each learner, with sections for their long-term and short-term goals. Educators are able to add to the Doc during each check-in, and the Doc can be shared with parents/caregivers as well.

3. For the purpose of goal setting, Check-ins should:
    1. Give educators a snapshot of where the learner is in regards to their Learning Plan (long-term goals).
    2. Provide insight into the daily/weekly goals the learner is setting (and how aligned these short-term goals are with the long-term goals).
    3. Highlight struggles the learner is presently encountering.
    4. Showcase examples of work, habits, and mindsets that should be celebrated!
    5. Allow educators to confidently communicate to learners and their parents/caregivers about the learner's progress.

Onboarding and Leading Parents/Caregivers on a Learning Journey

System Elements: Roles (parents as active participants)

Biggest Ripple Effect: Vision; Communications

What it is and Why:
Parents have their own expectations around how schools should "update" them on their learner's progress. In a learner-led environment, the responsibility is on the student to keep their parents abreast of their progress on their long-term and short-term goals. Parents will need their own coaching and resources to pull from as they navigate this transition from a school sending "report cards" to learners giving periodic updates on their own learning journeys. This isn't an exhaustive list, but here are some ideas for getting started:

1. Have an expectation that parents ask learners about their goals on Monday morning and to follow up on Friday afternoon by asking their learners how they progressed on their goals. This is a simple but important rhythm.

2. Give parents a list of questions to ask. Here are some to get started:
    1. What are the factors influencing the pace of progress at school? What are your biggest challenges?
    2. Are you on track to finish your learning goals this school year?
    3. What "right now" steps can you take to stay on track or get back on track, and what supports (from us and your educators) are needed?
    4. If you set a daily goal, and you finish that goal early, what will you do?
    5. What best motivates you to work toward a long-term goal? Extrinsic vs intrinsic motivators are both valuable.
    6. How will you keep this momentum throughout the school year?
    7. What's more important to you—making progress in your e-learning platform, or having a firm grasp on the material?
    8. How can you invest any extra time you have? Are there classmates you can help/mentor?
3. Communicate to parents/caregivers the process/expectations around Mid-Action and After Action Reviews. Expect learners to spend significant time walking their parents/caregivers through the review, field questions, and align on future plans together.
4. Host regular parent meetings. Once a month, we have Parent Coffees. We do some coaching/guiding around learning science and our model, facilitate parent connections, and provide resources parents can use to check-in with their learners.

The *bottom line*:

Students only spend on average about 18.5% of their waking hours at school. Schools cannot be the only place young people are practicing growing in their agency. Parents and caregivers play crucial roles in guiding children to shoulder responsibility for their choices. Habits of self-directed learning take even deeper roots when young people are supported by *more* caring adults (like coaches, mentors, spiritual leaders). As a school leader, design robust systems (Dream Teams, Mentorships, Social Capital Tracker, etc.) that can boost the number of caring adults that are supporting a young person's growth.

Modeling Goal Setting

System Element: Roles

Biggest Ripple Effect: Community Practices and School Culture; Curriculum, Pedagogy, and Assessment

What it is and Why:
As school leaders and educators, we are all on our own learning journey. How can your life experiences be a model and inspiration for learners at your school? We think it's really important to share our true selves—our thoughts, plans, ideas, and failures—with learners. Here are some ways you can build this sharing into your school culture.

How to do it:
1. Daily discussions. We have Socratic discussions at least twice a day in our classes. These are short (15-minute) group conversations with three distinct parts: an inspirational story, four or five Socratic questions, and a closing call to action. These are great opportunities for school leaders or educators to highlight an important part of their story (especially the struggles!).
2. World-class examples. What is an example of a time you (school leader or educator) set an ambitious goal that you made incremental progress toward meeting? Showcase

that thing (play that guitar, highlight that painting, show pictures of that experience).

3. Bring in parents and community members who have a wide variety of expertise and have them share the processes and products (especially as it relates to setting goals)!

Conclusion

Self-directed learners are made, not born (or maybe we are all born as self-directed learners, but quickly have that impulse schooled out of us). Daily goal setting is that small discipline that dictates how successful we will be in any endeavor. Those of us with lots of experience guiding our own work don't even realize how important goal setting is! It's often an invisible process. Before it becomes a "hidden" skill, though, it needs to be built through deliberate practice. When you watch a professional athlete take the court, field, or pitch, you don't see the hours and hours of small disciplines that led them to that moment. The rhythm and routine of goal setting is similar. Our more experienced learners aren't even aware of their goal setting. It comes naturally to them, taking a large learning goal and "breaking it down" into manageable, time-bound pieces. So, our suggestion is this: build goal setting into the fabric of the school. Cultivate it at every turn. Coach it and support it. Celebrate it. Communicate widely (to your team, learners, and parents/caregivers) about the importance of setting and reflecting on learning goals. Then, watch self-directed learning take hold.

References

Bellanco, J., Paul, A., & Paul, M. (2014). *Becoming self-directed learners.* Windy City Publishers.

Rogers, C. (1969). *Freedom to Learn.* C.E. Merrill.

6

Organizing for Student Self-Pacing

What if students had more control of their pace? What if they could work faster and graduate early? What if they could take extra time to build mastery and explore their own interests? We've worked with multiple public and private school educators and leaders who've successfully given students control of pacing. It's possible and well-received by students.

Before describing the how, it's helpful here to distinguish between traditional schools and learner-led environments. In the industrial age model of schooling, the pace is set. Even teachers have very little say about the pacing of a course. The edict usually comes from someone else, either school administrators, district leadership, or curriculum creators, as to what topic learners should be engaged with on which day. In fact, when we—and we imagine you—talk to teachers about what they want to do in their classrooms, they voice a similar frustration: we can't keep up with the pacing guides and there's no room in the schedule to do anything else. Alas, content or standards must be covered.

DOI: 10.4324/9781003489894-6

This rigorous pacing stems, in large part, from the cultures of standardized testing that have become the most meaningful metric in traditional schools. The test dates are set. The content is set. And so, the pace is set. Students are expected to cram the content into their brains so that they can regurgitate it on the test. Along the way, agency is stripped from learners and teachers about what they will explore at any given time. They are given two options: keep up or get left behind.

Self-directed learning flips this paradigm on its head. It doesn't start with some predetermined, fixed-pace curriculum. It starts with the goals that learners are making for themselves based on their interests and preferences. That's the starting line. Because the goals they are setting are *already* tied to a desired outcome, pacing then really comes down to three options. Option #1: at this pace, the learner is *on track* to achieve their outcome. Option #2: at this pace, the learner is *ahead* of where they need to be at this time and will achieve their outcome earlier than they anticipated. Option #3: at this pace, the learner is *behind* in achieving their outcome and it will take longer than they originally anticipated unless they change their pace.

You see the difference? In a self-directed environment, learners can still be behind on their work. The key difference between this environment and traditional school, though, is that the learner is behind on their *own* goals that they set for themselves and they have the power to adjust *their* pace if they want to. Their pathway is not determined, but flexible. They are in the driver's seat and can course correct along the way.

For those of us in traditional settings, the idea of student pacing may seem out of our hands. We have strict expectations on where students should be by certain milestones in the year. So, in those constraints, how do we empower learners to self-pace? Before we dive into some specific techniques, here are some general thoughts on how you as a school leader can empower your educators to navigate pacing in a traditional school environment:

◆ *Have educators identify their locus of control*: Given the expectations of pacing guides and the time constraints in a classroom, what pacing decisions are in the educator's control? During onboarding and professional development opportunities, guide your team of educators to identify the elements of pacing that they have control of. What we've observed is that teachers often have more agency than they realize. They assume that pacing is completely out of their hands and have rarely been asked to identify the decisions they do control. Examples of pacing decisions that educators (not administrators) can make are how the curriculum is covered, what the deliverables are, when they're due, and what's assessed.

◆ *Ask educators to name the barriers*: Classroom teachers are well-positioned to identify the obstacles they face in allowing students to pace themselves. Invite educators to feel safe in naming the barriers in their way. If creating greater student agency is a priority for you as a school leader, empower and encourage your team to highlight the obstacles they face that are beyond their control to address.

◆ *Find the wiggle room*: Look at the barriers identified by your classroom teachers. Which of those is in your locus of control as school leader? Report back to educators the barriers that you can mitigate and those beyond your control.

◆ *Start small*: Find small ways to open up learner self-pacing. Often, when it comes to conversations about self-directed learning, there is a misconception that it's all or nothing—that learners either have complete autonomy or none at all. That's a false dichotomy. With your team of educators, identify small but meaningful places where students can have some say in the pace of their learning.

◆ *Encourage learners to go deep, broad, or fast*: A significant consequence of all learners going the same pace is that high-performing students get bored and check out. If a student finishes their expected work, can they move ahead? Can they dive deeper into the material? Can they explore more broadly? Work with your classroom teachers to create options for students to go *deep* (work toward greater mastery of the topic), go *broad* (explore other, semi-connected topics), and go *fast* (move ahead to the next thing). Most curricular resources will have extension activities teachers can utilize with learners looking to go deeper.

◆ *Some concrete ideas*: Given the constraints of your environment, here are some tangible things you can try in any classroom.

   ◆ Give learners the syllabus. Include all deliverables and readings. Invite them to create their own pacing plan to meet all requirements.

   ◆ Flexible deadlines for deliverables, with incentives to turn in work earlier (some ideas: tiered grading, requiring an earlier deadline for A+ consideration; the opportunity to get feedback on an early draft and revise for a better grade; the option for learners to create their own passion project when they finish; opportunities for further leadership development or mentoring for learners who complete deliverables early).

   ◆ Give learners more choice in what is graded. Some learners might want the consistent feedback of graded homework and daily classwork. Some may choose to show what they know on the final project or exam.

   ◆ Schedule small blocks where learners can choose *what* they are working on and for *how long*. Given your constraints, you may have limited time to let learners set their pace. But even small moments of self-pacing give learners practice at goal setting, time management, and self-regulation.

A Story

Northern Cass School District in North Dakota has adopted a learner-led pathway. High school students can choose self-directed experiences or a traditional pathway. All middle school learners use the self-directed approach. Here's how it works in the high school. Students can replace any course with a self-directed Studio. So, for example, a student can choose to replace World History or English 10 with a customized project. A learning coach meets with students and asks them what they want to explore. What are they curious about? What problems in their community or in the world do they want to tackle? What skills do they want to build? Based on those interests, learners co-design a project with their coach. Then, the coach provides a list of the standards from the courses they are substituting. Together, they work to map the standards to the lessons and deliverables of the project. Once the deliverables are set, the learner creates a schedule with milestones and a culminating final project. Students typically work in six-week bursts, creating and delivering a customized project that infuses the requisite state standards. By co-creating the project and the schedule of deliverables, students stay in the driver's seat of their own pace.

Techniques

The following techniques are helpful in creating a culture where the pace of learning is determined by the learners themselves. Included in these techniques is helping learners create a big picture of the outcomes they want to achieve, teaching them skills to backwards map from those outcomes to smaller goals, creating systems and experiences that will prompt them to reflect on their current progress, and empowering them to pivot as needed.

Goal Setting and Self-Pacing

System Element: Community Practices and School Culture

Biggest Ripple Effect: Schedules and Routines; Roles

What it is and Why:
We've covered a lot of territory on goal setting. For good reason: it has positive ripple effects on student agency. Here, though, we want to highlight how the habit and practice of goal setting is directly tied to self-pacing.

How to do it:
1. Educators guide learners to understand their "Big Picture" goals. The main question learners need answered: *What do I need to do to move on to the next grade/level?* Students should have a firm grasp of everything they are on the hook for submitting, earning, doing in order to finish their own learning plan.
2. Break the school year into smaller time units. Does your school run on semesters, quarters, units, or something else?
3. Educators guide learners to "backward map" their goals. The main question learners need answered: *If I need to complete this goal by the end of the school year, how many pieces can I break it into?* It's helpful here to have metrics to use. For example, completing percentages of online courses, reading a certain number of books, logging a certain number of mentor hours, etc. How can learners *measure* their progress toward their "Big Picture" goals?
4. Parse the "Big Picture" goals into smaller and smaller pieces. Start with the school year. Then, a smaller unit (see Step Two). Then smaller still. Break the year into months, weeks, and days. A student should be able to say with

confidence, "If I do (small goal) every day, then I'll meet (large goal) by (deadline)." If a learner lacks that confidence or grounding, then the educator needs to guide them in building that "Big Picture" knowledge of their learning goals.

Give Students the Syllabus

System Element: Pedagogy, Curriculum, and Assessment

Biggest Ripple Effect: Schedules and Routines; Roles; and Communications

What it is and Why:
One way to give learners control of pace is to let them work through material as fast as they want. Perhaps you had a college class where the professor distributed the syllabus on the first day, with all the assignments, deadlines, and readings clearly articulated and encouraged you to—if you really wanted to—work ahead. Why couldn't a middle or high school teacher take a similar approach? That's just what Jason Hughes and his team of math teachers did at Hall County High School in Gainesville, Georgia. They provide their learners with a syllabus outlining the deliverables for the course and unleash them to work as quickly as they want. Students that have a firm grasp on the material (as showcased in mastering assessments) don't have to wait for the rest of the class.

How to do it:
- ◆ Guide your educators to create a syllabus for a course or even a unit within the course. The syllabus should highlight the major deliverables, assignments, due dates, and required readings/resources.
- ◆ Create incentives for learners that want to work ahead. Maybe if they finish early, they get to design a passion

project? Maybe they can matriculate to new material? Maybe they "unlock" student leadership within the school and spend time mentoring others?

Something to consider:
This technique of giving learners the syllabus and letting them work ahead isn't intended to *reinforce* the idea that school is all about checking boxes and getting grades. A key part of getting away from the "checkbox" approach to school is to build a culture where learners clearly see the relevance in their work. How many of us have heard our learners ask "Why do I have to learn this? When will I ever use this?" We may brush off the questions, but they're valid. By providing a syllabus and letting learners tackle it, we're saying: here's the material you need to know and master in order to move on to the next grade or level, *show us what you know*. The emphasis isn't on the checkboxes; it's on the learner's ability to use the checkboxes as a springboard to mastery. A learner that can do this (self-regulate and self-pace according to a syllabus) is well-prepared for whatever work their college or career will throw at them.

Embedding Choice in the Schedule

System Element: Schedules and Routines

Biggest Ripple Effect: Facilities; Pedagogy, Curriculum, and Assessment; Roles

What is it and Why:
Schedules (daily, weekly, and longer-term) will be peppered throughout the book. We've mentioned schedules before, but in this chapter, we'll focus on schedules as a tool for learners to set their own pace. Schedules are inherent constraints that we as school leaders and educators use to ensure we're giving learners adequate time and practice to cultivate the skills, knowledge,

and mindsets of our Profile of a Graduate. Within the confines of a set schedule, though, are plenty of places for students to "own" their own time and pace of work.

How to do it:
1. Publicly post daily and weekly schedules (as well as any longer-term events, deadlines, or milestones) in the classroom and refer to them often.
2. In the daily schedule, create blocks of time that belong to the learners. Some schools have a daily block where students can choose what they're working on (Red Bridge in San Francisco calls these blocks Deliberate Practice). Maybe they spend an hour on math, read for thirty minutes, then spend the rest of the time editing an article. Some schools (like Crossroads College Preparatory in St. Louis) have created a weekly block where learners self-select a project to work on. Whatever the cadence, give learners a chance to *choose a task that aligns with their own learning goals*. Give them small practices at setting their own pace. What is on us as leaders and educators is guiding them to evaluate and deeply reflect on their current pace as it relates to their goals. The next technique is helpful for prompting that reflection.

"Holding up a mirror"
System Element: Roles (teachers as Guides)

Biggest Ripple Effect: Community Practices and School Culture

What it is and Why:
What is the role of an educator when it comes to monitoring and tracking a learner's pace? This is a nuanced approach, and one quite different from typical teacher-centered classrooms. We call it "holding up a mirror," and it's a technique that can

be utilized *within* a variety of other techniques we have or will highlight (Check-ins, Socratic discussions, Learner-led conferences, etc.). It is what it sounds like: the educator merely serves as a "reflector," guiding learners to take stock of current data and pivot accordingly. This may sound simple, but it's actually a ninja move that takes skill to do well. We'll give you a starting place.

How to do it:
1. It's important to generate a lot of meaningful data. Some helpful things to track:
   1. Time (How are learners spending their time? This is especially helpful on e-learning platforms that track engagement.)
   2. Progress/Completion units (e.g., a percent of an e-learning course).
   3. Words/Paragraphs/Pages (How much writing are you students doing?)
   4. Books (How are learners tracking their reading?)
   5. Completed Courses (Where are learners when it comes to completing their Learning Plans?)
   6. Feedback/Evaluations (from peers, educators, and external experts)
2. Present the data to learners.
3. Guide them through reflection of the data. Some helpful questions:
   1. What do you notice?
   2. This data represents your progress to date. At this pace, will you meet your goals by your deadline?
   3. Is there anything you need to do more of? Less of?
   4. On a scale from 1 to 5, how easy is it for you to get into flow and knock out your work? What do you need to change to get to a 5?
4. Present world-class examples. A great way to "hold up a mirror" is to offer a great example of *the thing* (essay,

prototype, pitch deck, etc.). Have learners compare their work to a masterwork and identify gaps. Then, bring the conversation back to pace.

Freedom Levels

System Element: Community Practices and School Culture

Biggest Ripple Effects: Tech and Tech Infrastructure (for tracking); Roles; Continuous Improvement Mechanisms

What it is and Why:
Self-directed learning is a journey. We've argued elsewhere that there's a pathway that people follow as they become more self-directed (Collier, 2022). A question many leaders have as they begin or transition to a learner-led model is how to appropriately support students as they grow in their ability to self-direct. A simple but helpful technique is to offer a scaffolded approach to learner agency, where students earn greater freedom as they show they can take responsibility for themselves and their work. We call these "Freedom Levels."

How to do it:
1. Create tiers or "levels." The highest level grants students the widest range of freedom and choice. Decide how many levels you want to create (this can vary by age group).
2. Create requirements for each level. Make them crystal clear. Post them in the classroom and communicate them widely with students and parents. Some ideas for requirements:
   1. Academic Progress. If you have a Badge system, this is a helpful way to track and celebrate students as they earn a certain number of badges. If you don't have a Badge system, you can use another metric of

completion: units, levels, grades, etc. The goal here is to create Freedom Levels that align with how "on track" a student is in regards to their own learning goals.

2. Peer feedback. We talk elsewhere about 360 Feedback. A helpful metric is to have students anonymously give their peers feedback on how well they're showing up, holding to the class promises, and contributing to the learning culture. Whatever metric you use, you need something that doesn't merely gauge academic progress. A learner shouldn't be able to achieve the highest Freedom Level if they're not abiding by the agreements the community has made.

3. Make the requirements such that Freedom Levels are hard to attain and easy to lose. Moving up in Freedom Levels should be a big deal to learners. It should be celebrated. And, if they fail to keep/adhere to the requirements, it should be possible to move down in Freedom Levels as well.

4. Make the rewards something students care about. The new freedoms "unlocked" when a student moves up in Freedom Levels should be highly prized. Some things we've found success in (again, this varies on age): choosing seating, choosing groups, listening to music, earning extra break time, mentoring younger learners, and taking greater leadership in the classroom.

5. Handoff as much of the process to learners as possible, but ensure due process. Like any system, Freedom Levels can be gamed. The role of the educator is to ensure fairness and fidelity to the system, and tweak (with learner input) as needed.

An example:
Red Bridge, a K-8 school in San Francisco, California, has a system of "Autonomy Levels." Their autonomy levels are decoupled

from academic progress. Instead, learners advance through autonomy levels by displaying habits of self-directedness and self-regulation.

Learner-Led Conferences

System Element: Community Practices and School Culture

Biggest Ripple Effect: Roles; Facilities; Communications

What it is and Why:
Most schools have some version of a parent–teacher conference. In many cases, the learner isn't even present. Or if they are included, they are a passive audience, listening to adults discuss their learning. We take a different approach. We do invite parents/caregivers in for conferences, but these are learner-led meetings. The learners themselves present their goals, their progress, their obstacles and struggles, and their plans for the future. The learner then fields questions from their parents/caregivers and the educator. The educator can present their own insights and perspectives, but the heart of this meeting is putting the student in the driver's seat of the conversation.

How to do it:
1. The logistics of scheduling can be the most difficult part of conferences. Work with your team to design a process that works. The goal should be to have at least 20–30 minutes for each learner.
2. Have learners prepare beforehand. A template can be helpful (like the MARs and AARs we've discussed). Build time into the schedule for them to prepare. They should be able to clearly articulate their "Big Picture" learning goals, their progress on those goals, and their current pace (i.e., "At this pace, I'm on track to finish (goal) by (deadline).").

3. Keep the learner at the center. It can be tempting in conferences for the adults (parents/caregivers and educators) to dominate the conversation. Create and maintain a culture at your school that positions the student as (1) the most knowledgeable of their current pace/progress and (2) the one with the responsibility to make any pivots or changes.

4. End with action steps. Based on the conversation, what should happen next? Make sure that everyone leaves the conference with clear expectations about what actions the learner will take.

Conclusion

We often hear frustration about the "pace" of learning in traditional classrooms. Some learners feel left behind. Some are bored and feel like they're wasting their time. Educators are stressed with trying to keep up with predetermined pacing guides, while also trying to be responsive to learners that are behind or ahead. Schedules are impossibly full, for students and teachers alike. Add to this that most reform movements tend to add *more* to the mix, not less. Teachers and learners are expected to do more work, learn new systems, engage with new curriculum, and be assessed by "new" metrics.

All of this has led to an epidemic of anxious students and burned-out teachers.

By no means are we arguing that self-pacing is a panacea that can cure all the ills of a broken system. But we do believe that putting the pace of learning *in the hands of the learner* is one of the most revolutionizing moves a school can make. The anxiety of students trying to keep up with the rat race? Gone. The boredom of students who really want to fly in their learning but are "held back" by the pre-set pace? Gone. The stress of teachers trying to keep everyone on track while adhering to some arbitrary pacing guide? Gone.

It's not easy. And it requires a reimagining of how we typically do "education." But it's possible. If students are given meaningful choices (see Chapter 4), are empowered to set their own learning goals (see Chapter 5), and are unleashed to go at their own pace (this chapter), then watch out: your school is well-situated to cultivate a crop of curious, creative, critical thinkers ready to shape the world.

Reference

Collier, C. (2022). Becoming an autonomous learner: Building the skills of self-directed learning. *Journal of Transformative Learning*, *9*(1), 111–120.

7

Empowering Students' Rule Making

There's a world where children are made to fit schools. There's a world where schools are made to fit children. This chapter explores the latter.

Let's start with some real examples of high school learners at The Forest School: Sarah Grace used her school's resources (time, people, courses of study, materials, etc.) to launch her acting career. Logan leveraged his school to get his pilot's license and gain acceptance to engineering school. Lauren, to graduate early. Josiah, to practice leadership. Oswin, to learn animation and deepen his storytelling expertise. Sophia, to figure out what she wanted to do and eventually launch her military career.

In some ways, this chapter is a step back. In most schools in this country right now, kids are passively sitting at desks listening to adults answer questions they didn't ask and following rules they had no hand in making. In the first half of this book, we've focused on the first part of that problem. The techniques in the previous chapters can help a school center the learner in

DOI: 10.4324/9781003489894-7

the whole learning process. Now, it's time to shift our focus to rulemaking.

Elsewhere, we've made the argument that Industrial Age model schools run on the twin tracks of *compliance* and *accountability* (Kenner et al., 2020). Accountability, which limits the autonomy of learners and teachers, has been tied to a spike in anxiety, educator burnout, and disengagement from students and teachers alike (Gallup, 2013; Ingersoll et al., 2014; Simon & Johnson, 2015). Likewise, compliance is aimed at negating freedoms in the classroom. In its landscape analysis, the Institute for Self-Directed Learning argued that:

> Compliance-driven cultures can also damage and stagnate executive function skills in children in other ways because compliance can be understood as the ways in which adults are often viewed as the keepers and disseminators of knowledge, and creators of the rules, and students as the passive recipients who must "comply" by their standards and rules and therefore do not prepare learners to think critically, plan intentionally and make good choices.
>
> (Kenner et al., 2020, p. 10)

This approach to schooling has led to an epidemic of dependent learners. Hammond (2014) argued that dependent learners "struggle because we don't offer them sufficient opportunities in the classroom to develop the cognitive skills and habits of mind that would prepare them to take on the more advanced academic tasks" (p. 13). Schools designed with accountability and compliance as their guiding principles do not foster independence; they extinguish it.

This is an old critique of schooling. Paulo Freire argued back in 1970 that: "Education either functions as an instrument which is used to facilitate integration of the younger generation into the logic of the present system and bring about conformity, or it becomes the practice of freedom, the means by which men and women deal critically and creatively with reality and discover how to participate in the transformation of their world" (Freire, 1970/1996, p. 16).

That begs the question: what are young people getting more practice at, conformity or freedom? Most of the tools and training available to school leaders and teachers is about the former, about how to efficiently achieve conformity via the old staples of compliance and accountability systems. There are very few tools in the leader's or educator's toolbox about cultivating freedom in our schools.

That's where this chapter comes in.

A key part of a learner's experience at school *should be* growing in the skills of self-governance, democracy, and conflict resolution. Most students are getting very few "at bats" with any of those skills. If you are a leader looking to cultivate agency in your school (and since you've made it this far in the book, then we assume you are) then you're going to need a whole new toolbox to shift the culture from one of conformity to one of where learners grow in the "practice of freedom," as Freire put it. The following techniques will guide you and your team to clearly articulate the boundaries (via an Honor Code), equip you to guide learners into creating compelling rules for their classrooms, and will empower you to hand off the responsibility for enforcing the rules to the learners themselves.

A Story

In Ohio, Columbus City Schools have begun using Student-Led Restorative Practices (SLRP; which we will highlight as a technique in this chapter) as a way for learners themselves to mediate conflicts between peers. Students volunteer to receive SLRP training, then they become the primary mediators in peer-to-peer conflicts. The district is still early in the process of training and implementing SLRP, but students note a decrease in fights and a boost in empathy. One student reported: "This really helped us open up…During the community circles, I saw how many people were willing to be vulnerable in front of their classmates. Most people didn't hesitate to share and we found that a lot of us are going through the same things" (Siefert, 2023).

Peer-mediated conflict resolution works (Johnson et al., 1995; Lyubansky, 2016). Often, when adults are involved, learners are defensive. Maybe even resistant. They often feel like a solution is being imposed by authority figures. When peers are mediating the conflict resolution, though, there is a greater emphasis on community ownership of the process and co-creation of the solution. The parties in the conflict have a chance to share their perspectives and hear each other. Their peers are trained to facilitate. Both sides create an agreement to abide by. The beauty of this process is that the learners own it, from start to finish.

Techniques

Honor Code

System Element: Vision

Biggest Ripple Effect: Community Practices and School Culture; Roles

What it is and Why:
An "honor code" is pretty self-explanatory. Many organizations and institutions have a clearly articulated code that highlights the ethical guardrails for their members. In this chapter, we'll present many techniques for guiding learners to create their own rules. First, though, it's crucial that your leadership team takes a stance on the clear non-negotiables of your learning environment.

How to do it:

1. Use your mission, vision, and design principles as a "North Star" as you create your Honor Code.
2. Put clear "stakes in the ground" around your non-negotiables. Consider these three focuses in your Honor Code:
   1. **Safety**: As school leaders, our first and greatest priority is to ensure the safety of our learners, educators, and family members. This means *physical* safety, as well as *mental* and *emotional* safety.
   2. **Respect**: Make it clear that your expectation is that everyone will be respected at your school.
   3. **Responsibility**: A learner-driven environment puts more responsibility on learners, not less. Create an Honor Code that explicitly states that learners are responsible for their words and actions and will be held accountable.
3. With your leadership team, draft a thoughtful Honor Code.
4. When you have a draft in-hand, take it to the community. Ask parents/caregivers for feedback. Present it and discuss it with learners. Make necessary revisions.
5. Communicate it widely and post it publicly. No one should be unclear about the boundaries.

Contract of Promises

System Element: Community Practices and School Culture

Biggest Ripple Effect: Roles

What it is and Why:

With the Honor Code in place, each class can then roll up their sleeves and get to work creating their own rules for governance. A Contract of Promises is just that: a list of all the agreements the students are vowing to uphold. The Contract should be brief enough that it's easy to post on the wall, recall, and reference often.

How to do it:

1. Devote serious time to creating it! Some learner-centered schools spend the first month of school ideating and co-creating the Contract. Make it a priority by giving it the time it deserves.

2. Use liberating structures to ensure everyone's voice is heard in the process of creating the Contract. Some great resources can be found at https://www.liberatingstructures.com.

3. Strike a balance between being broad versus specific. Look for themes. For example, the contract can address distractions in a broad enough way that the agreement can be applied to many different scenarios.

4. Encourage experimentation! Have learners pick and choose "agreements" that they will abide by for a day or week. Get feedback on how that went and whether they feel that those particular agreements would be helpful for the whole class to follow.

5. Bring in outside experts. We bring in the mayor of our town, contract experts, and professional negotiators to give students feedback on the early drafts of their governance structures.

6. Memorialize the agreed-upon rules in a "Contract." After weeks of iteration, our classes agree upon the rules that will govern their spaces by creating a Contract of Promises. We have a public moment where the learners sign their names to this contact and agree to be held accountable to it.

7. Make the Contract visible. Post it on a wall in the classroom. Refer to it daily.

8. Hold up a mirror. When the class isn't living into the promises they made to each other, simply call out the behavior and refer to the contract. Bring them into the decision-making process. Ask, "What should we do, change our Contract or change our behavior?" Students want to operate in a well-structured, well-governed space. Give them opportunities to address their short-comings in self-governance and make improvements as a community.

Rules of Engagement

System Element: Community Practices and School Culture

Biggest Ripple Effect: Roles

What is it and Why:
Discussions are a key component of a learner-led school design. Students gather for group conversations multiple times throughout any given day. The "Rules of Engagement" are the agreed-upon norms that structure our conversations. Like the Contract of Promises, the Rules of Engagement should also be learner-created.

How to do it:
1. Use the same protocols from the previous technique (Contract of Promises) to create the Rules of Engagement for group discussions. It will be helpful to build these at the same time.
2. Keep it simple! Learners should be able to easily understand and memorize them.
3. Post them prominently in the classroom and refer to them before *every* discussion.
4. Give learners control. A common technique we use is to ask, "What three Rules of Engagement should we focus on this time?" at the beginning of a discussion. Have

student volunteers keep an eye out and hold the group accountable for those Rules of Engagement. This keeps the educator from being the enforcer and empowers learners to facilitate their own discussions.

Allow Learners to Experience Natural Consequences

System Elements: Community Practices and School Culture

Biggest Ripple Effect: Roles; Communications; Curriculum, Pedagogy, and Assessment

What is it and Why:

There are consequences for breaking "rules" and "promises." It can be difficult, as a school leader and educator, to align on appropriate responses to student infractions. Over-enforcement and punitive consequences can quickly make a school feel like a prison, void of freedom and agency. On the other hand, an overly lax response communicates to students that the rules don't matter. In that setting, the structures of self-governance break down. Finding the balance is a bit of a Goldilocks move and may take some trial and error. Here are some tips we've found helpful.

How to do it:

1. Guard the Honor Code (see above). The Honor Code should ensure safety, respect, and responsibility. There should be real, immediate consequences for a student that threatens the safety of others or is disrespectful to peers or adults. As a leadership team, create these consequences, communicate them clearly to students and parents/caregivers, and enforce them consistently.

2. Have students create the consequences for breaking the Contract of Promises (see above). The Contract is the list of agreements that a particular class of learners are making with one another. Since the Contract itself is learner-made, the consequences should likewise be created by

students. In our experience, learners are better than adults at creating accountability structures that they want to comply with. If you find that the class *is not* holding each other accountable to the Contract of Promises, then this is a time to "hold up a mirror." Guide the students through a conversation about the Contract and consequence system. Ask them if either should be amended. Have them give ideas for next steps.

3. Don't be afraid to let it fall apart. It can be tempting, as an adult, to want to step in and "clean up" a messy class culture. Maybe the students aren't upholding their Contract. Maybe the consequences aren't having the desired effect. Maybe the systems aren't working. Our advice: keep "holding up a mirror." Keep prompting the conversations. Keep asking the question. Learners want to be in a structured, well-governed space. They don't want chaos and disorder. Sometimes, though, they need to experience the chaos to realize it's not what they want. If an adult is constantly intervening and trying to "fix" the class culture, students will be conditioned to rely on adult action and oversight. Once they learn it's on them, though, learners will take action. They'll govern their space. They'll uphold the Contract. Leaders will emerge. That leads to the next technique: Council.

Council

System Element: Community Practices

Biggest Ripple Effect: Roles

What it is and Why:
A learner-led classroom is a great laboratory for democracy. Students learn how to make rules together, hold each other

accountable, navigate differences of opinion, and resolve conflict. The educator has a role to play in all of those things. First, to ensure safety and respect (i.e., the Honor Code). Then, to provide protocols, structures, and world-class examples for students to learn from and utilize if they wish. The goal of the educator in self-directed learning, though, is to get out of the way *as quickly as possible*. That means handing off key leadership responsibilities to students and entrusting them with the care and keeping of the class culture. Our approach to this is a student leadership committee we call Council. Here are some ideas on how you could structure it in your setting.

How to do it:

1. How will your Council be chosen? Will there be a democratic election where students choose their Council members? Is Council appointed by the educator? What are the requirements for being on Council (maybe tie eligibility to a Freedom Level)?

2. Start small. Put Council in charge of one or two systems (e.g., Freedom Levels, Conflict Resolution). Train your leaders on these systems and entrust them with oversight. See Council members as leaders-in-training that need coaching and mentoring.

3. Ensure due process. All learners should feel empowered and protected by the systems and structures. With a Council of their peers in charge, some learners may feel slighted, targeted, or treated unfairly. Have a robust system for all learners to air grievances, make appeals, and seek educator support.

4. Hold Council *even more* accountable. Being a leader in the class means a learner is held to a higher standard than their peers. Expect your Council to go above and beyond adhering to the Contract of Promises and positively contributing to the class culture.

Student-Led Restorative Practices

System Element: Community Practices

Biggest Ripple Effect: Roles

What it is and Why:
Similar to Council (see previous technique), Student-Led Restorative Practices (SLRP) puts conflict resolution in the hands of learners. In Ohio, Columbus City Schools has four high schools utilizing SLRP. Students in these four high schools can take leadership training in restorative practices and they themselves take care of all first-tier discipline issues.

How to do it:
To learn about this particular approach, read more about Student-Led Restorative Practices (www.studentledrp.org). Here's the *why* behind their work: "The strongest improvements in student outcomes emerge at the confluence of a highly engaged learner and a highly effective educator. The ideal culture and climate, then, is one that creates learner engagement by maximizing student agency, autonomy, and empathy. And it's one that supports educator effectiveness by freeing them up to focus on instructional delivery. Both of these strategies are brought to life through Student-Led Restorative Practices."

Celebrations

System Element: Community Practices

Biggest Ripple Effect: Schedules and Routines; Communications

What is it and Why:
We've mentioned Celebrations before, and the old adage that "You cultivate what you celebrate." It's helpful to mention it again here, in the context of learner-created rules and norms. If you want to cultivate a positive culture in your classrooms,

one with high standards where learners consistently hold each other accountable, then the educators and school leaders need to intentionally be recognizing and celebrating these things. How do you celebrate your student leaders? How do you recognize the learners that show up every day and do the hard work of self-governance? How do you publicly honor a student who fell short of the Contract of Promises but then did the hard work of making amends with the class? Intentionally create an environment that celebrates the mindsets, habits, and behaviors it aspires to cultivate.

How to do it:

1. Shout Outs. What if learners had dedicated time every school day for giving gratitude to one another? This could be a simple but powerful way to build a culture of gratitude at your school. Lead by example. As educators and leaders, publicly "shout out," or acknowledge, learners that are living into the Contract of Promises. Celebrate moments when students learn from their mistakes. Build a culture that sees failure as a teachable moment, not a defining characteristic of who a person is.

2. Love on your leaders. Being a leader in any environment is hard, draining work. It can be even more exhausting in learner-led spaces, when being a leader may come at the expense of some social capital. As a school leader and educator, find ways to breathe life into your student leaders. Celebrate them. Reward them. Coach them up. A temptation in self-directed learning is for some student leaders to "check out" of the community element. They keep their head down, get their work done, and don't worry so much about the class culture. Empowering these learners to take responsibility not just for themselves, but for the class culture as a whole, means you need to be intentional about celebrating them and protecting their energy.

3. Celebrate your team. Publicly cheer your educators, administrators, and leaders for embodying your core values.

4. Cheer on the community. The world is full of everyday people doing awesome things. Recognize and honor the ways your parents/caregivers, neighbors, and other community members are exemplifying the ideals of your school.

Something to consider:

These sorts of celebrations aren't meant to be a "student or teacher of the month" kind of recognition. They should be authentic. One strong way to build authenticity is through storytelling. When celebrating someone, be it a learner, an educator, or someone in the community, share stories. Speak about how their character was highlighted through their words and actions. Invite others to share stories as well.

Conclusion

What if kids didn't think of "school" as a place that managed and controlled them? What if, instead, they saw school as a world they got to shape and create? What if, at school, students got *real* practice at making and upholding community promises, navigating across lines of difference, finding compromise, and resolving conflict? What sort of mindsets, skills, and habits would that develop within them? What sort of world would they go out and shape someday?

At the beginning of this chapter, we quoted Freire and the idea that schools are places that either practice freedom and conformity. Our question to you: how much practice are students getting in your school environment practicing freedom and self-governance? Practicing freedom is hard, messy work. The techniques in this chapter are just small ways to get started. They're insufficient on their own. The work must be driven by a simple but profound belief: young people are capable.

References

Freire, P. (1970/1996). *Pedagogy of the oppressed*. Penguin Books.

Gallup (2013). *2013 Gallup student poll: Overall U.S. report*. Gallup, Inc. http://www.gallupstudentpoll.com/174020/2013-gallup-student-poll-over-all-report.aspx

Hammond, Z. (2014). *Culturally responsive teaching and the brain: Promoting authentic engagement and rigor among culturally and linguistically diverse students*. Corwin Press.

Ingersoll, R., Merrill, L., & Stuckey, D. (2014). Seven trends: The transformation of the teaching force. *Consortium for Policy Research in Education*. http://eric.ed.gov/?id=ED566879

Johnson, D. W., Johnson, R., Dudley, B., Ward, M., & Magnuson, D. (1995). The impact of peer mediation training on the management of school and home conflicts. *American Educational Research Journal*, 32(4), 829–844. https://doi.org/10.2307/1163337

Kenner, B., Carlson, R., Raab, E., & Smith, A. (2020). Self-directed learning: A landscape analysis and recommendations for transforming educational practice. *Choice Filled Lives Network*. Retrieved May 30, 2024, from https://static1.squarespace.com/static/5e386db54376d45a8a76e551/t/5ff48bdb392438636260503e/1609862108655/Self+Directed+Learning+-+A+Landscape+Analysis+-+Final.pdf

Lyubansky, M. (2016). Outcomes of restorative circles programs in high school settings. *Psychology of Violence*.

Siefert, K. (2023, September 13). *Student led program aims to resolve conflict in Columbus City Schools*. WSYX. https://abc6onyourside.com/news/local/student-led-program-aims-to-resolve-conflict-in-columbus-city-schools-aj-crabill-restorative-practice-social-emotional-training#

Simon, N. S., & Johnson, S. M. (2015). Teacher turnover in high-poverty schools: What we know and can do. *Teachers College Record*, *117*(3), 1–36.

8

Nurturing Exploration

A key foundation of self-directed learning is that children are *naturally* curious. They want to know things. They want to understand. They want to make meaning of the world. You don't have to *force* a child to want to learn. This curiosity is already etched into their being. Aristotle made this claim millennia ago. He argued in the *Metaphysics* that "all men by nature desire to know" (Aristotle, 1908, p. 1). Humans are innately curious beings. To Aristotle, that was the starting point of education: the individual curiosities of a person to know and name the world around them.

Somewhere along the way, though, those that shape education systems have lost that belief. They stopped seeing children as curious beings who *wanted* to learn. Instead, students needed to be *motivated* to learn. They needed systems for accountability. They needed rigorous assessment. They needed to be prodded along predetermined pathways with ever-evolving "sticks and carrots." Somewhere along the way, education leaders lost sight of the fact that each child is a genius, *willfully* able to guide their own learning.

DOI: 10.4324/9781003489894-8

To move back toward an agentic approach to learning is a hard pivot. It takes a drastic mindset shift for leaders, educators, parents, and students. This shift, though drastic, is not impossible. It just takes a different set of tools than traditional education.

Let's start with a thought experiment: envision creating a school focused on cultivating dependent students. Yes, you read that correctly—*dependent* learners who rely heavily on others for guidance and decision-making. While this concept might initially strike us as unsettling, let's temporarily set aside our judgments and explore how such a school could be developed.

First, our hypothetical institution would prioritize structured learning environments. Students would navigate carefully orchestrated steps, minimizing the need for independent problem-solving. We'd enforce limited autonomy, furnishing students with explicit rules and guidelines for every facet of their educational journey. To further restrict freedom, we'd implement rigorous daily routines, rigidly dictating students' schedules.

When it comes to the curriculum, we'd decree the subjects they study, leaving little room for choice. To bolster their dependence, we'd offer abundant academic and emotional support resources, ensuring they could lean on assistance whenever needed. Information sharing would be closely guarded, concealing planning processes, policy decisions, and disciplinary verdicts to keep students in the dark and reliant on authority figures.

Continuous supervision would be paramount, minimizing opportunities for independent problem-solving. Classrooms would exude conformity, celebrating uniformity with well-defined learning objectives, discouraging individuality and independent thinking. Direct instruction would dominate, emphasizing teacher-centered learning to restrict independent exploration. Assessments would focus on finding singular correct answers, discouraging diverse perspectives and creative solutions. Risk-taking and experimentation would be discouraged, sheltering students from the consequences of their choices. Predefined pathways would limit exposure to options, discouraging vocational exploration. Ultimately, this approach would solidify students' dependence on authority figures, reinforcing the notion that authority possesses the right answers. Critical thinking and independent inquiry would be discouraged in favor of conformity and reliance on external guidance.

Ok, whew, the thought experiment is over.

Of course, that was just an exercise, but the trouble is this—an imaginary educational design that would cultivate dependency in its graduates dangerously resembles the current design of most K-12 schools across our country. So, let's design something different. Let's design schools that encourage learners to follow their own natural inquiries. The techniques in this chapter can help us pivot in that direction.

The Pathway of Self-Directed Learning

We would be remiss at this point to not address a common critique of self-directed learning. It goes something like this: some children are able to be self-directed (they come into a learner-led environment already displaying strong habits of self-direction) and some children aren't (they lack the skills and capabilities of directing their own learning). We reject that view.

We believe that all children have the potential to guide their own education. Co-author Dr. Caleb Collier published a peer-reviewed article titled "Becoming an Autonomous Learner: Building the Skills of Self-Directed Learning" (2022). In it, he conducted a meta-analysis on decades of research into self-directed learning. What emerged from the research was a common pathway that people follow as they become more autonomous in their learning. There are four distinct (but overlapping) phases.

Phase 1: The Desire to Learn
Learners must first build a *desire* to learn, which researchers see as a combination of motivators, a growing sense of self-efficacy,

and a combination of environmental/social factors (basically, they have their needs met, feel safe, feel like they belong, and feel like they can make a positive contribution to a group). This goes back to Aristotle's argument that all humans desire to know, that we are all innately curious and want to make meaning of the world. Unfortunately, this curiosity dwindles unless it is consistently fed. To help rekindle it, our role as leaders and educators starts with the learner: what do they want to know? What questions are they pondering? If they could explore any topic, master any skill, build any knowledge, what would it be? That's where we start: the natural curiosity of the learner. Once they have a desire to learn, they don't need to be prodded into a learning journey. They seek it out.

Phase 2: Resourcefulness

Once that foundation is laid, learners can move to the next stage of self-directed learning: learner resourcefulness. Once they have a desire to learn, students then take stock of next steps. They do cursory research. They gather resources. They ask questions. The habits in this phase are basic self-regulation strategies—the ability to choose to do something challenging (like learn a math concept) instead of something immediately gratifying (like chatting with friends). People develop resourcefulness over time through habitual practice. This phase of self-directed learning cannot really take root without really building the foundation of desiring to learn.

Phase 3: Initiative

The third phase is learner initiative. After a learner wants to know something and they've started gathering resources, then it's time to get started. This aligns with the vision of self-directed learning we have laid out in this book: the ability to identify a task to complete or problem to solve, make a plan, set goals, evaluate progress, and revise the plan as necessary. These are skills built through habitual practice. The claim can be made that initiative has both internal and external qualities. A person may possess some sort of drive, or innate motivation to undertake a learning task. Another possibility is that the invitation comes from an external source: a problem to solve, a job skill to master, or a treasure to seek.

Phase 4: Persistence

A student gets curious to learn something new (Phase 1). They begin putting resources and a plan together (Phase 2). They take the first steps (Phase 3). Then? Well, then things get harder. Perhaps they encounter new knowledge and skills that push them out of their comfort zone. Perhaps they get stuck and aren't sure how to move ahead. Perhaps they lose a bit of the motivation that got them started. This is when Phase 4 kicks in: students learn how to *persist* through obstacles and challenges and see their learning project through to completion.

Takeaways

Decades of studies in the field have identified the pathway that people take to become self-directed learners. Interestingly, researchers found that individuals who started at Phase 1 and tried to move directly to Phase 4 had a much harder time completing their learning journeys. Learners that moved through the pathway one phase at a time were more likely to finish what they started *because they developed the skills, mindsets, and habits* of each phase along the way. Our point is this: anyone can become a self-directed learner; it just takes dedicated practice.

A Story

Tara Westover's (2018) bestselling memoir *Educated* chronicled her upbringing by parents who were religious extremists.

Her childhood was spent helping her father work in a junkyard and assisting her mother with midwifery. She taught herself to read and write, but lacked exposure to higher-level math, science, and history. She decided she wanted to go to college, but when she picked up a SAT prep book, she realized how little of the material she actually knew. She felt defeated.

But she didn't give up. She set to work teaching herself algebra and calculus, setting her own goals and pulling together whatever resources she could find. She eventually scored high enough on her SAT to gain acceptance to Brigham Young University. It was not until she stepped into history class at college that she encountered important historical concepts like slavery and the Holocaust. So, she would spend her nights and weekends at the library, brushing up on history while her peers experienced their college lives.

Notice the pathway of self-directed learning at work. First, Tara has a *desire*. She wants to go to college. To get to college, she needs a high enough SAT score. All the learning that happens next happens as an offshoot of her desire to learn. Then, she gathers resources. She gets an SAT prep book. Then she gets started. She practices. Then the obstacles start mounting: there's so much she doesn't know! But she doesn't quit. She perseveres. She sees the challenge through. Then, when she gets to college and realizes she's behind her peers on important historical concepts, she begins the cycle again. She connects her desire to resources. She uses those resources to learn. She perseveres when it gets hard. Eventually, Tara is invited on a fellowship to Oxford University.

You see, she had chalked her childhood education up to a wasted experience. The reality, though, is that she was slowly building the habits and mindsets of a self-directed learner. And when the time came for her to tackle a problem, she employed those habits to slowly and methodically work through the pathway. Tara had learned how to teach herself anything.

Techniques

Real-World Project-Based Learning

System Element: Curriculum, Pedagogy, and Assessment

Biggest Ripple Effect: Bridges and Partnerships; Roles

What it is and Why:
Let's face it: school work can be boring. Worse, the work we're expecting students to complete is often not *relevant* to their own learning goals, nor does it address any *real* need in the world. The work lives in the vacuum of the class and dies on the teacher's desk. Students are really good at seeing this. They know when work is just *busy work*. They can tell when an assignment is just something to do for a grade. It doesn't have to be that way. Project-Based Learning (PBL), tied to real-world needs, is a great way for learners to see the immediate relevance of their work. When done well, students stop asking "Why do I have to learn this?" and instead take the mindset of "How can I use what I've learned to solve this problem?" Here's how to get started.

How to do it:
1. Use Design Thinking (a human-centered approach to problem solving and innovation) in your PBL creation process. Here's how:
   1. Identify people in your community who are experiencing a real problem (these are your "users").
   2. Guide your learners through a process of conducting empathy interviews and doing research so that they can adequately understand the problem the user is experiencing.
   3. Through an iterative process, learners prototype solutions and get feedback from experts in the field. They utilize this feedback to continue to improve their work.

4. Learners present their final products to the users in a public exhibition and receive an evaluation from the user, experts, and visitors. They later reflect on this feedback and make goals for future learning.

2. "Right size" the project for your learners and your time constraints. Some schools can devote multiple time blocks each week to a PBL unit. Some may have less. Design the project around your constraints. Be sure your learners will have adequate time for "sense making" (and potentially empathy interviews), time to explore and research, time to experiment and iterate, time to receive feedback, and time to create a final product.

3. Bring in the community. We're firm believers in having "porous walls." Past projects have included our learners designing a roller coaster for a nearby theme park, a multi-use path for our city, a community garden for our neighborhood, and a haunted house for local residents.

The Bottom Line:
This chapter is all about unleashing natural exploration in learners. A fun and engaging way to do that is to present them with a real problem and let them choose the resources and approach to solving it.

Socratic Discussions
System Element: Curriculum, Pedagogy, and Assessment

Biggest Ripple Effect: Roles; Schedules

What it is and Why:
Socratic dialogue has been an educational approach since...well, Socrates. The ancient Greek philosopher had a habit of asking questions. And when his students asked questions, he replied with *even more* questions. A common trait among us educators is

that we like to answer questions. We like to share knowledge. We like to teach, via direct instruction and lectures, because we're passionate about our areas of expertise. This isn't a bad impulse. It's part of what drove many of us to education in the first place. But notice who is at the center of this approach: we are. The so-called "Sage on the Stage" model of education is how many of us were taught. Socrates, though, models a different approach. Through Socratic Discussions, educators use the power of storytelling and question-posing to drive the curiosity of learners.

How to do it:

1. Intentionally design and schedule Socratic discussions. Elsewhere, we highlight techniques like "Rules of Engagement" to lay the norms and expectations for these discussions. This shouldn't feel like an "add-on" to a lecture, but a separate experience governed by specific expectations.

2. Set a time limit (we've found a lot of success with short 15-minute discussions).

3. Choose a relevant topic or theme.

4. Find and tell an inspiring story. This is a great way to "hook" learners into the discussion and ignite their curiosity.

5. Create 4–5 Socratic questions. A good Socratic question:
   1. Has no clear right or wrong answer.
   2. Prompts deep thinking and debate.
   3. Often forces a choice. (We call these A/B questions. For example, "Would you choose to do (A) or (B)?" This forced choice invites learners to make a clear stand on a position.)

6. Facilitate the conversation. For a 15-minute discussion, a good expectation is that the educator would spend 3–4 minutes telling the story and asking the questions, and that the learners would use the rest of the time discussing and debating.

7. Use liberating structures (https://www.liberatingstructures.com) to ensure that every learner has their voice heard.

8. End the discussion with a call to action that is directly relevant to the work learners are doing.

Take it further:
The "Advanced-Player Mode" of Socratic Discussions is for educators to stay in Socratic mode all the time! That means no lectures, no direct instruction, and no answering of questions (except with thoughtful questions to provoke learners to find their own solution). Again, this is not an option for all educators in all settings, and we're not making the case that there isn't a place for direct instruction or answering questions. Rather, the challenge is to "de-center" yourself as the educator and holder of knowledge and "center" the curiosities and problem-solving skills of your learners.

Curating Relevant Resources

System Element: Curriculum, Pedagogy, and Assessment

Biggest Ripple Effect: Budget, Operations, and Logistics

What it is and Why:
A key role of an educator in a self-directed learning environment is to curate resources. This is different from a teacher in a traditional classroom that assigns textbooks and worksheets and requires a different mindset from the educator. Think of it this way: if a professional were to undertake a project on the topic at hand, where would they go to get started? These resources need to be relevant (they are directly tied to helping learners understand the topic deeper), easy to engage with and understand (videos/infographics tend to be better than academic texts), and varied (multiple types of resources in different modalities and reflecting various points of view).

How to do it:

1. How do you learn something new? Where do you go? Start by building your own library of recommended resources. Ask your team to contribute.

2. Tap your network. When we undertake a learning project, we ask experts in our community for resources. If our community is lacking in the necessary expertise, we tap our wider network by posting on our socials, reaching out to other education leaders, or making some cold calls. One of our roles as school leaders and educators is to leverage our networks so that we can pass the best, most-relevant learning resources along to our learners.

3. Be broad. Provide a variety of viewpoints and perspectives. Don't rely on single sources.

4. Give primary sources. As much as possible, give students access to original works, not explanations and overviews from secondary sources.

5. Curate good resources, but equip learners to find their own. Finding, vetting, and synthesizing information is a key skill for all learners. Guide them in building these muscles on their own.

Free Play and Exploration

System Element: Community Practices and School Culture

Biggest Ripple Effect: Schedules and Routines; Facilities

What it is and Why:

This is pretty self-explanatory. Young people learn through play. This is a key tenet of many approaches to early childhood education (Montessori, Reggio Emilio, etc.). The focus falls away in upper elementary and middle school. We think it's important that children of all ages have time to freely explore their own interests. This looks different across age groups, but the bottom line is this: *build time into the schedule for learners to freely play and explore.*

How to do it:
This is not really a "how to," but rather encouragement: find small ways to allow unstructured play. This could be a field trip, outdoor experiences, or some flexible Physical Education blocks.

Learner-Designed Courses
System Element: Curriculum, Pedagogy, and Assessment

Biggest Ripple Effect: Roles; Schedules and Routines

What it is and Why:
We've talked about Customizable Learning Plans before. The focus of this chapter, though, is nurturing a learner's independent exploration. A great way to do that is through customizable learning plans. What if learners not only could customize their learning pathways, but also their learning outcomes? What if they could receive school credit for learning about whatever they wanted? We've been privileged to see some amazing examples of Learner-Designed Courses: Acting 101, Intro to Guitar, Architecture, Chess, Automotive, and a Health and Wellness course that became our official High School PE credit at The Forest School. The courses that learners design become available to other learners to take, which adds value to the course creation process.

How to do it:
1. Is it possible for learners to design and "pitch" their own courses at your school for credit? If it is, then here are some ideas for your process! If not, then is it possible for learners to pitch their own units of study *within* existing courses? If so, then share this possibility with your team of educators.

2. Provide ways for learners to customize their learning plan from the youngest ages. Learners that gain experience building their own learning units in elementary grades will be that much more adept at it when they're older. Below is the "checklist" we use with learners

An example:

Here's the checklist we give our learners to guide them as they create their own courses to pitch:

> *If you could spend ~50 hours learning anything you want, what would it be?*

PITCH CHECKLIST

As you design your pitch, the following things must be true about your learning experience:

☐ *You think your learning plan will be fun and challenging*

☐ *Your learning plan includes multiple readings, writing tasks, "world class examples," and reflection activities (Note: a "world class example" can be anything that industry experts think is worthy of imitation)*

☐ *Your pitch includes SMART and WOOP goals, roles, plans, and timelines where appropriate*

☐ *Your learning plan includes elements that are directly connected to your interests and/or purpose statement as well as elements that are intentionally disconnected from your interests (to expand your horizons)*

☐ *Your learning plan somehow requires the use of research skills and analytical skills*

☐ *Your learning plan includes a small project that makes you use your learning to help a real person or persons*

☐ *All of the learning activities you design for yourself take 40–50 hours to complete*

○ *Your learning plan costs the school $0 and your parents an amount you agree upon (free is best)*

○ *Your learning plan has a title that colleges will like*

A panel of two or three adults will assess your learning plan against the checklist above. All three adults must check every box in order for your plan to be approved. Expect to pitch multiple times before your plan is approved.

Using Mastery-Based Transcripts

System Element: Curriculum, Pedagogy, and Assessment

Biggest Ripple Effect: Community Practices and School Culture; Roles; Tech and Tech Infrastructure

What it is and Why:

There's a movement in many schools away from arbitrary grades and toward assessing for competency-based mastery. Many schools use a Mastery Transcript (see exemplars at www.mastery. org) that captures and catalogs their evidence of mastering the outcomes in their Portrait of a Graduate. This Mastery Transcript is what is sent to college admissions offices. The beauty of earning Mastery Credits is that learners can bring any evidence from any point in their lives, in or out of school. This allows us to cultivate a learning culture that sees and celebrates the whole person, but it also unleashes each learner to freely explore their own interests. Here are some tips to get started.

How to do it:

1. Create your Portrait of a Graduate (see Chapter 3).
2. Create your system of Practicals (see Chapter 10).
3. For each outcome in your Portrait of a Graduate, create a single-point rubric.

4. For each outcome in your Portrait of a Graduate, guide learners to compile evidence of mastery (from any time of their life, in or out of school).

5. After each Practical, give learners feedback according to the single-point rubric. Our expectation is that students will usually need to present evidence multiple times to pass a Practical. Our response (with appropriate feedback) is either "Yes, you've clearly shown mastery" or "Not yet, you have more work to do."

Providing Choice in Task, Tools, and Assessment

System Element: Roles

Biggest Ripple Effect: Curriculum, Pedagogy, and Assessment

What it is and Why:
In Chapter 4, we discussed techniques for promoting student choice. As we think about nurturing exploration, it's important to revisit the simple concept of choice. Every single day, in a myriad of ways, students will either make choices themselves or have choices made for them by someone else. A key design question in a learner-led environment is: "What decisions can I hand off to learners?" Our encouragement is to hand off as much decision-making to students as quickly as you can.

How to do it:
Review the techniques for promoting student choice (Chapter 4), goal setting (Chapter 5), and self-pacing (Chapter 6). In general, school leaders and educators can nurture exploration by giving choice in:

- *Task*: How often do students get to choose what they are working on?
- *Tools*: How often do learners have choice in the resources they will utilize?

◆ *Assessments*: How often do learners get to choose how their learning is assessed?

By building in plentiful opportunities for students to choose their tasks, tools, and assessments, schools can cultivate curious learners who have mastered the skills to explore their own interests and teach themselves anything.

Conclusion

We started this chapter with a hypothetical thought experiment: designing a school to intentionally cultivate *dependent* learners. Sadly, many schools are stuck in that same cycle, churning out graduates who have had little practice at following their own curiosities. What if school was different? What if each and every learner had various opportunities to freely explore their interests? What if these interests were reflected in their learning through customized portfolios and mastery-based transcripts? What if each graduate was a self-directed learner, skilled in the abilities to teach themselves anything?

The techniques in this chapter are just starting places, but they are concrete, tangible ways to infuse natural exploration into any school design. Combine these techniques with those in other chapters, like goal setting, pacing, and assessment, and a culture of self-directed learning will quickly take root.

References

Aristotle. (1908). *Metaphysics* (trans. W. Ross). Clarendon Press.

Collier, C. (2022). Becoming an autonomous learner: Building the skills of self-directed learning. *Journal of Transformative Learning*, *9*(1), 111–120.

Westover, T. (2018). *Educated*. Random House.

9

Embracing Productive Struggle

One of the major inequities of traditional schooling is that different learners are "tracked" onto various predetermined tracks. Schools continue to disproportionately place marginalized students (usually kids of color or from lower socioeconomic strata) into lower-level courses when compared with their peers (Thornton, 2023). Even with education reforms that seek to provide more equitable learning environments, systems that govern the sorting of students into various learning tracks remain largely intact. The outcome is that some learners will be placed on "academic" tracks (often carrying labels like "gifted" or "advanced") while other learners, deemed unable to meet the rigor of an academic track, are placed in "remedial" classes. The work in these lower-level courses is mostly rote memorization and fails to provide productive struggle.

Productive struggle encourages students to engage in challenging tasks, promoting deep learning and resilience. It allows children to confront and solve problems independently or with

DOI: 10.4324/9781003489894-9

minimal guidance, enhancing their understanding, problem-solving skills, and persistence. Research in education has identified several benefits of productive struggle, including improved academic achievement, development of a growth mindset, and enhanced problem-solving skills. Here are some of the benefits of allowing students to experience productive struggle:

- *Development of Deep Learning*: Engaging students in productive struggle helps in the internalization and deeper understanding of concepts. According to research, when students struggle with material within their zone of proximal development (ZPD), they are more likely to construct meaningful connections and retain information longer.
- *Promotion of a Growth Mindset*: Carol Dweck's research on mindset highlights the importance of embracing challenges and persisting in the face of setbacks (2006). Productive struggle fosters a growth mindset by teaching students that intelligence can be developed through effort and perseverance.
- *Enhancement of Problem-Solving Skills*: Studies suggest that students who engage in productive struggle develop stronger problem-solving and critical thinking skills. By navigating challenges and exploring multiple solutions, students learn to approach problems flexibly and creatively.
- *Improvement in Academic Achievement*: Research indicates that students who experience productive struggle in their learning process often show improvements in academic achievement. This approach encourages active learning and engagement, which are critical for academic success.
- *Development of Self-regulation and Persistence*: Productive struggle teaches students how to manage their emotions and motivations during challenging tasks. This self-regulatory skill is crucial for academic and personal success.

◆ *Cultivation of Resilience and Grit*: Angela Duckworth's research on grit underscores the value of persistence and passion for long-term goals (2016). Productive struggle helps in cultivating these qualities by encouraging students to persist through difficulties.

A Story

At The Forest School, learners are ultimately in charge of their own goals, pace, and progress. So, what happens when they fall behind? Sometimes they rebound quickly. We meet with them and their parents and point out that at their current pace, they will take longer to complete their goals, which would mean they would be behind when it came time to advance to the next level. One of our seniors, Josiah, realized he wouldn't graduate on time. He already had options for his next steps: college acceptances to consider, as well as acceptance to an influential "gap year" program. The sticking point was that he was behind on meeting his graduation requirements, which put those options in doubt. What did he do? He got to work. He made a plan to finish his learning plan. He worked nights and weekends when necessary. He put his full effort into catching up and finishing. On graduation day, Josiah took to the stage to address those gathered for commencement. "Learn from me," he told his classmates. "Don't procrastinate. Don't put your work off. It's not fun to do it the hard way."

What's inspiring about his story is that Josiah experienced an "aha" moment. He realized his learning (and meeting his school requirements) was ultimately up to him. No one was going to do it for him. He had mismanaged his time, played or got distracted when he should have been making steady progress on his goals. Then he had to make up for it. It was a stressful few months leading up to graduation. But he persevered. Pushed through. And that experience—engaging in that productive struggle—provided valuable lessons he could take into college and his career.

Techniques

Allow and Celebrate Failure

System Element: Vision

Biggest Ripple Effect: Community Practices and School Culture; Communications

What it is and Why:

Fear of failure causes learners to limit their options, take fewer risks, mismanage their time, while increasing their stress, burnout, and depression and lowering their emotional wellbeing (Borgonovi and Han, 2021). The focus on the metrics of grading (i.e, GPAs and standardized tests) have undercut students' willingness to make (and learn from) mistakes in their work. We've all had experiences of learning from failure. We know the value that mistakes have in the learning process. Yet, we've created an education system that penalizes (rather than celebrates) learners willing to take risks in their work. The good news is that you can build a culture that embraces failure as a building block to success!

How to do it:

- ◆ Expect iteration. For all projects, have students turn in a number of drafts. Celebrate the growth that happens from the rough draft to the final version.
- ◆ Grade less. Not all homework and classwork needs to be graded. Give learners practice at material without the expectation that everything has to be perfect.
- ◆ Encourage trial and error. If a student doesn't know what to do (in a math problem, for example), can they try and figure it out? Will they be penalized for trying and getting it wrong? Or, will they be able to try, fail, and try again? When a student asks a question about how to do

something, build a default response of "What have you tried?" As schools leaders and educators, embracing the concept of "Not yet" empowers students to see learning as *productive*, as a journey that may be difficult, but it's ultimately worth it in the end.

◆ Use single-point rubrics to focus on a demonstration of mastery while cultivating a growth mindset.

◆ Prompt reflection and meta-cognition. Guide learners to self-assess and identify the gaps in their knowledge. Empower them to gameplan their own solution to shoring up needed skills and knowledge.

◆ Publicly celebrate risk-taking. Shout out the learners who take big swings, even if they have big misses. Many learners will be hesitant to try and fail because they don't want to be shamed. Take the shame out of risk taking by celebrating learners who courageously tackle unknown challenges.

Allow Learners to Experience Natural Consequences (as quickly as possible)

System Element: Curriculum, Pedagogy, and Assessment

Biggest Ripple Effect: Communications; Roles; Community Practices and School Culture

What it is and Why:
Often, the consequences students experience in school can seem arbitrary, irrelevant, and not immediate. Increasing the choices learners have in the classroom also increases the need for learners to experience the natural consequences of those choices *as quickly as possible*. We learn from consequences, both positive and negative, and experiencing them impacts the decisions we will make next. As you increase agency in your school, here are some ways you can think about creating quick "feedback loops"

for learners to experience the natural consequences of their choices. As educators, we often struggle with this because we see our own success tied to the success of learners. Throughout this book, we'll continue to argue for self-differentiation: the ability for educators to untangle their own performance from the performance of their students. Ultimately, a learner is responsible for their own learning. An educator's role in a self-directed environment is to attend to the learning design, provide learners with clear processes, resources, and protocols, allow young people to make meaningful choices and experience real consequences, and prompt learners to take stock of their own learning and reflect on what adjustments they might need to make.

How to do it:

- ◆ Degrees of freedom. Learners (especially ones that have been in traditional models of school a long time) will likely need scaffolded experiences of freedom. As you implement more choice and freedom in your classroom, a direct consequence of abusing that freedom could be losing it (for example, choice in seating or task).
- ◆ Accountability systems. As you engage with your students to create the rules and norms of your classroom, also task them with building systems of self-governance. What happens when a learner falls short of the class agreements? Young people are really good at identifying accountability systems with "teeth." Engage them to co-create the systems, then follow them with fidelity.
- ◆ "Opting out" should be less fun than "opting in." In some learner-centered settings, young people have the option to opt out of certain learning activities. If you are providing students with the choice to participate, then make sure the alternative to not participating is boring by comparison.

◆ Group work should mirror the real world. When we were students, it wasn't uncommon for one or two people to carry the team in group work assignments. In the real world of work, there are consequences to falling short in your duties and responsibilities. Each learner should be "on the hook" for public and private deliverables. And if they shirk responsibility, they should be held accountable to their teammates.

Challenge Zone

System Element: Curriculum, Pedagogy, and Assessment

Biggest Ripple Effect: Communications; Roles; Community Practices and School Culture

What it is and Why:
Building off of Vygotsky's work on the "zone of proximal development," the Challenge Zone is a visual and pedagogical framework for supporting learners as they engage with deep, meaningful learning.

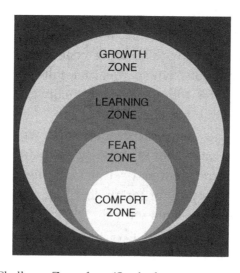

FIGURE 9.1 The Challenge Zone, from iStock photo.

Posting the image of the Challenge Zone (or Challenge Donut) in your classroom is a great way to help learners frame their thinking when taking on difficult work. The Challenge Zone is a bit like the Goldilocks fairytale: some work is too easy, some work is too hard, and some work is just right. The center circle is the Comfort Zone. Work in the Comfort Zone is easy. It's familiar. It's boring. Learners working in this zone are prone to disengage and check out. The outer circle is the Panic Zone. This work is too hard, too unfamiliar. Learners in the Panic Zone are anxious. Stressed. They procrastinate and distract themselves rather than engaging with the work. In between the Comfort Zone and Panic Zone is the sweet spot: The Challenge Zone. This work is just outside a learner's current level of skills and knowledge, meaning that it provokes *growth*. They have to level up. Build on a foundation. Sharpen a skill. Learn something new. This is Vygotsky's "zone of proximal development." Our role as school leaders and educators is to design learning experiences that guide learners into their Challenge Zone *while* coaching them up to self-reflect and assess where they are in the Comfort, Challenge, Panic Zone spectrum.

How to do it:
1. Post the visual in your classroom. Explain it. Refer to it often, in group discussions and one-on-one conversations.
2. Give learners regular practice at identifying which zone they're in.
3. Create flexible scaffolds.
    1. If a learner is in the Panic Zone, what can they do? Can they seek out a mentor? Are there additional (more foundational resources) they can refer to? Is there flexibility with the pace of their work (maybe they take longer) or their deliverables (maybe they submit something different)?
    2. If a learner is in the Comfort Zone, how can you *turn up* the difficulty? Can they go faster and move onto

something else if they can display mastery? Can they mentor someone else? Can they extend their learning by doing a deeper dive into the topic?

4. Provide parents and caregivers with Comfort Zone visual and language so that they can (1) understand the approach and (2) use the language in the conversations they have with their children.

5. Use the Wellington Index (see Figure 9.2) to gather learner feedback. This is a quick, easy way to have students access where they are. The x-axis of the chart gauges a learner's *interest* toward an activity (from "hate it" to "love it"). The y-axis gauges the level of *challenge* they feel in an activity (from "unchallenging" to "challenging"). High-interest, high-challenge activities are in the "engaged" quadrant. High-interest, low-challenge activities are in the "entertained" quadrant. Low-interest, high-challenge activities are in the "grind" quadrant. Low-interest, low-challenge activities leave students feeling "bored." A good feedback routine for educators is to have this chart on the board and have learners mark where they are after every activity. The goal is to have all learners in the "engaged" quadrant. Use the chart and the visual data it represents to have class discussions about how to boost the interest and challenge of the activities.

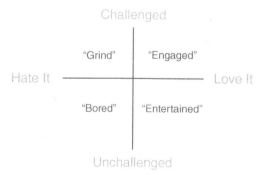

FIGURE 9.2 The Wellington Index, from The Wellington School.

The Learning Pit

System Element: Curriculum, Pedagogy, and Assessment

Biggest Ripple Effect: Communications; Roles; Community Practices and School Culture

What it is and Why:
Like the Comfort Zone, the Learning Pit is a useful visual for highlighting productive struggle.

Post this image in your classroom and use it for discussions and one-on-one check-ins. Use it to build a growth mindset. When learners say "I don't get it…I'm stuck…I'm confused," redirect them to reframe as "I don't understand *yet*." The downward slope of the learning pit represents how we feel when we're overwhelmed. It feels like sinking. At times, it feels hopeless. *But that's part of the process!* The beauty of self-directed learning is that young people realize *it's on them* to take on the challenge and climb out the other side. That's not to say that school leaders, educators, and caring adults don't have a responsibility to

FIGURE 9.3 From *The Learning Pit* by James Nottingham (2024).

support and encourage. But the metaphor of the Learning Pit is that deep learning happens when students embrace the challenge and persevere to get through to the other side. Our responsibility as caring adults is to guide learners to find and utilize supports that will help them make it out of the pit.

How to do it:

1. Post the image in your classroom and refer to it often.
2. Cultivate a growth mindset. Here are some questions to use with learners feeling stuck:
    1. "What strategies have you tried?"
    2. "Who have you asked for help?"
    3. "Is anything distracting you?"
    4. "Have you ever been stuck before? What helped then?"
    5. "Do you know what skills you need to practice or knowledge you need to gain?"
    6. "Do you need to adjust your goals or set new ones?"
    7. "Why is learning [this topic] important?"
3. Celebrate all stages of the Learning Pit! Sometimes, we only focus on celebrating learners that make it to the other side of a learning challenge. Acknowledge those that are in the early stages and those in the thick of it. Celebrate it when a learner feels stuck *but keeps going*. Celebrate resourcefulness and perseverance.
4. Share the Learning Pit image with parents and caregivers. Equip them with language to use as they talk about learning challenges with their children.

Degrees of Freedom

System Element: Community Practices and School Culture

Biggest Ripple Effects: Tech and Tech Infrastructure (for tracking); Roles; Continuous Improvement Mechanisms

What it is and Why:

A key part of growing from childhood to adulthood is an increase in the amount of freedom you have over your own life. As parents and caregivers, we seek to give our children greater levels of autonomy the older they get. Many students, though, are not given real, meaningful freedom before they enter college. The result? Often a frustrated freshman year as they quickly learn the skills of self-regulation and time management. What if all students experienced real freedom from their youngest years in school? What if they had meaningful choices about their own education, and learned the skills and habits of managing their freedom as well? A way to provide that practice is a graduated system of autonomy.

How to do it:

1. Create levels of freedom, with the lowest level being the most teacher-directed and the highest level being the most student-directed.
   1. *Examples of the lowest level*: students work in assigned seats and on assigned tasks.
   2. *Examples of the next tier*: students have a choice in seating, but still work on assigned tasks.
   3. *Example of the next tier*: students choose seating and have flexibility in what they're working on.
   4. *Example of the highest tier*: students have the highest amount of freedom, which may include moving around the room, choosing work, self-selecting times for "brain breaks," and choosing seating.
2. Make the levels and the requirements for achieving each level clear. Post it on the classroom walls.
   1. Requirements can include consistency in work (are learners doing their work?), quality in work (are learners motivated to improve their work?), and

adherence to class promises (are learners contributing positively to the classroom culture?).

2. Create a metric for each requirement so it's easy for learners to know where they are in the process.
3. Create a time horizon for assessing levels. Do learners move up or down levels every week or month?
4. Much of the process can be overseen by learners, but the role of the educator is to ensure fairness, consistency, and equity.

The bottom line:

Creating a tiered system of freedom is meant to be a tool that encourages students to take on more and more autonomy. This scaffolded approach is especially helpful for learners new to self-directed environments. Like any tool, though, a system like this could become another list of boxes to check. If any system you create that was originally designed to boost agency becomes another system that learners are dependent on, feel empowered to get rid of or redesign the system.

Provide Curated Resources, Scaffolded Steps, and Recommended Recipes

System Element: Curriculum, Pedagogy, and Assessment

Biggest Ripple Effect: Roles; Community Practices and School Culture

What it is and Why:

It's common for all of us to experience anxiety when given a high level of autonomy. Researchers call this the "dizziness of freedom" (Schwartz, 2004). When learners are given meaningful choices in their work, indecisiveness can be a by-product. Students can get *stuck* in their decision-making. A helpful way to "right size" this productive struggle is to provide a "menu of options" learners can quickly choose from. Here are some ideas.

How to do it:

1. When giving learners a choice in task, provide them a short list of options to choose from ("Would you rather do option A, B, or C?").
    1. *A tip*: Planning for multiple options in a lesson can be time-intensive for teachers. A way to lighten this load is to have similarity across all options in terms of the topic, but the differences could be in modality. For example, "Will you write a story, record a podcast, or create a short presentation?"
2. When giving learners freedom to research or design a project on their own, provide a list of vetted resources they can easily access.
3. For large, multi-step projects: provided scaffolded steps that learners can choose to follow. Some may want to work on the project in their own way, but others will appreciate having a recommended "step-by-step" approach.
4. When provided students choice in a project, provide world-class examples as recommended "recipes." The prompt could look something like this: "For your end of unit project, you may want to consider (this example), (this example), or (this example)." For each example, give further details (recipes) learners could follow if they wanted to do similar work.
    1. To create even further autonomy, be open to learners pitching their own ideas for a final project. A teacher in Pike County, Georgia, shared an example of two students who partnered together to pitch, design, and paint a mural on the school that connected to the learning standards of their history course.

Manage Goal-Setting Partners and Mentors

System Elements: Roles

Biggest Ripple Effect: Schedules and Routines; Community Practices and School Culture

What it is and Why:

Support systems are crucial for creating a culture of "right sized" productive struggle. Use systems like Goal Setting Partners or Mentors to provide learners with peer support. We discuss these specific techniques elsewhere, but here it's important to point out that your class community is a valuable resource. Here's how to structure systems to cultivate peer support:

How to do it:

1. The most important part here is to build a strong classroom culture. Do students feel a sense of responsibility to help and support each other? Do learners feel safe and supported enough to ask for help? Tend to your class culture first and foremost.
2. As you build your protocols for Mentors or Goal Setting Partners, create a series of questions that learners ask each other when they meet. Some examples:
   1. "What are you most frustrated with in your work right now?"
   2. "What have you tried?"
   3. "What are you going to try next?"
   4. "Would you like some support?"
3. Celebrate when learners seek help from and give help to a peer.

Hold Clear Boundaries

System Element: Roles

Biggest Ripple Effect: Communications

What it is and Why:
There can be a misunderstanding that learner-led spaces have "hazy" or unclear boundaries. Some critiques of self-directed learning is that it gives learners too much freedom, resulting in a *Lord of the Flies*-type of chaotic environment. That's not the case! Learner-led environments—just like any classroom—are governed by well-defined boundaries. The difference between these classrooms and less agentic spaces is that the learners have a key role in creating (and an expectation to uphold) the boundaries. It's important that school leaders and educators continue to empower learners to take on that responsibility. It's also crucial that the adults in the space ensure that the boundaries are upheld with fairness and equity. The primary responsibility for school leaders and educators is to ensure that all kids are safe (physically, mentally, and emotionally) and that everyone feels respected in the environment. To do that, learners will look to the adults to clearly set and hold boundaries to protect the community.

How to do it:
1. Have clear documentation (like an Honor Code) of expectations and consequences.
2. Be consistent in upholding the consequences for breaking the Honor Code or Class Promises.
3. Ensure that all learners feel protected by the school and don't have to shoulder problems of safety or disrespect on their own. It is true that in learner-led spaces, learners have more agency in holding themselves and others accountable to the class-made rules. However, this does not mean that adults have any less responsibility to ensure safety and respect.
4. Embrace practices of restorative justice. Learners will fall short of promises and expectations. We all do at some point. While still holding young people accountable, create systems that aren't merely *punitive*, but are designed

to be *restorative*. The end goal of the systems is to protect the community and class culture while providing pathways for the offending party to make amends and be restored to the community.

5. Use "levers of control." Educators in learner-led classrooms may have different roles than traditional teachers, but they still have multiple "levers" for holding students accountable. As a school leader, empower educators to identify and utilize these levers to maintain the health of the classroom. Examples of levers:

    1. *Freedom*: How much freedom and choice do learners have? Educators work within the systems of the classroom to reward more or further constrict freedom of learners. Upholding the Honor Code and Class Agreements is a requirement for advancing to greater freedom levels.

    2. *Seating*: Educators have ultimate say over where students work in the classroom. Learners not living into the Class Agreements may be temporarily "siloed" in their work, having to sit in an assigned place under the educator's supervision.

    3. *Schedule*: Educators control the schedule. Using the schedule as a "lever" means that some students may have different expectations for what they're working on when.

    4. *Privileges*: Like freedoms, privileges within the classroom can be earned. Some schools use incentives like extra break time or earned field trips. Learners "earn" this privileges by adhering to the Class Promises and meeting their learning goals.

Utilize Learning Science

System Element: Curriculum, Pedagogy, and Assessment

Biggest Ripple Effect: Roles

What it is and Why:

We're always growing in our understanding of how the human brain works, especially how it develops over time. As our knowledge of learning science develops, we gain insights into tweaks we can make in education design. It's on us, then, as school leaders and educators to be responsive to new understandings of the science of learning. A resource we have found helpful is Transcend's Designing for Learning (Charlot, Leck, & Saxberg, 2020). Transcend identifies four key factors that influence learning: cognition, motivation, identity, and individual variation. We'll briefly explore these with hands-on tips on maximizing them in your environment.

How to do it:

- ◆ *Cognition*: Cognition refers to the way we learn new stuff, store it, and retrieve it for application. Here are Transcend's tips for boosting cognition for your learners:
  - ◆ Focused Attention: Learners are more engaged with and focused on learning experiences that they see relevance in. Have a clear *why* for every activity you give to learners.
    - ◆ *Some tips*: When you are introducing a new topic, be intentional about why learners are encountering it and how it connects to their overall education. To pivot towards self-direction, have learners identify their own "learning targets" in the material.
  - ◆ Manageable Cognitive Load: Like the Challenge Zone, learners learn best when they are not overwhelmed by the amount of new material to learn. Create scaffolded, iterative processes for students to learn something new, bit by manageable bit.
    - ◆ *Some tips*: Guide learners to build on previous knowledge (e.g., using a KWL chart, highlighting their Knowledge, Wonderings, and Learnings).

Use resources like the Challenge Zone or Learning Pit in check-ins with learners to pinpoint their struggles. Provide high-quality, timely feedback on early drafts to celebrate work and give encouragement for growth areas.

◆ Meaningful Encoding: We remember things that we learn in *memorable* ways. Create engaging ways for learners to experience new material that also builds on prior knowledge.

  ◆ *Some tips*: When starting a new lesson or unit, create an exciting "launch" to create excitement and buy-in from learners. Throughout a unit, create ways for learners to have hands-on, multimodal experiences to build knowledge. Have learners present their learning in public showcases that add public value and create a memorable experience around the learning.

◆ Effective Practice: Give learners plenty of "at bats" at new skills and knowledge in focused intervals and across a variety of contexts.

  ◆ *Some tips*: Present learners with familiar concepts in different contexts. For example, take a math concept (like fractions) and create multiple experiences (e.g., baking or making slime) that give them practice outside of worksheets or e-learning platforms.

◆ High-Quality Feedback: Provide learners with timely and targeted feedback so they can iterate on their work.

  ◆ *Some tips*: Bring in multiple avenues of feedback, including self-reflection, peer feedback, and expert evaluation. Prioritize giving learners targeted feedback over grades and provide them with opportunities to iterate and improve their work.

♦ Metacognitive Thinking: Prompt learners to reflect on their own learning and identify strengths to celebrate and weaknesses to shore up.

    ♦ *Some tips*: End every learning activity with a reflection prompt. A simple but effective question is "I used to think...but now I think..." Create exit tickets for learners to reflect on what they learned, their main takeaways, and their lingering questions.

♦ *Motivation*: Motivation is the overlapping factors that impact a person's willingness to start and persevere in a learning project. Here are Transcend's principles for boosting motivation:

    ♦ Value: Do learners see the value in the learning experience? Is it meaningful? Provide a clear *why* to build student buy-in for the activity.

        ♦ *Some tips*: Ask learners to identify the value in each and every activity. Have them connect it to their own interest and personal goals. Show that you value the learner's time and attention by not giving busy work and by connecting every assignment to a relevant outcome.

    ♦ Self-efficacy: Do learners see themselves as competent and capable in the project? Do they see a process toward mastery? Guide learners to reflect on (and tap into) their self-efficacy in the learning project.

        ♦ *Some tips*: Helpful reflection questions to use: "On a scale from 1 to 10, how confident are you in your ability to do this project? What would help you gain confidence and get to a 10? What have you tried? What resources have you gathered? Who have you asked for help?"

    ♦ Sense of Control: Do learners have meaningful choice in the learning activity? Is it something they are being forced to do, or do they have autonomy within the project? The more you can boost choice within the learning design, the more motivated students will be to take it on.

- ◆ *Some tips*: This book is full of techniques to boost a learner's sense of control. Start small. Give learners meaningful choice in what or how they're learning and how they are assessed.

◆ Constructive Emotions: Like the Panic Zone or the Learning Pit, students engaged with new, challenging work can be overwhelmed. They learn best, though, when they're not anxious but rather working from a place of self-efficacy and confidence.

- ◆ *Some tips*: Use Check-ins to help learners identify stressors and assist them in creating a plan to overcome the challenges.

◆ *Identity*: Each learner brings themselves to the learning experience. As education designers, it's on us to build environments and experiences that invite learners to explore and express their full, authentic selves. Here are Transcend's tips:

- ◆ Self-Understanding: Guide learners through identity work so that they grow in their understanding of who they are and how they learn.

  - ◆ *Some tips*: Create meaningful assignments designed to prompt learners to deeply reflect on their identity. There are a ton of ideas out there: guide learners to create family trees, interview family members, create self-portraits, identify their strengths and passions, create videos or songs that highlight their identity, etc.

- ◆ Sense of Belonging: A key part of being school leaders is cultivating an environment where everyone feels a deep sense of belonging. Learners that feel excluded or othered will disengage from the learning and the community.

  - ◆ *Some tips*: Use a Belonging Survey to gain insight into how learners are feeling in the classroom. These are anonymous surveys that provide glimpses into whether each learner feels welcomed and included in the class culture. Use the data to have conversations as a class about how you can intentionally boost the sense of belonging for everyone.

- ◆ Navigating Identity Threats: If a young person feels like their identity isn't protected, then school ceases to be a safe space for them. Part of the hard work of building a diverse, inclusive culture is helping young people on individual and group levels navigate the complexities around identity threats.
  - ◆ *Some tips*: Have clear boundaries that protect and safeguard everyone's sense of physical, emotional, and mental safety. Have clear processes that students can use if they are feeling targeted or threatened. Respond to these instances swiftly and decisively.
- ◆ *Individual Variability*: Young people are complex. We, as school designers, must attend to and celebrate this complexity. Here are tips from Transcend:
  - ◆ Life Experiences: Each student that enters your doors has their own unique lived experiences. They learn best when their unique advantages and adversities are seen, understood, and responded to.
    - ◆ *Some tips*: Invite parents and caregivers into the classroom to share their own family stories and cultural backgrounds. Have learners create a family tree or genealogy and present it in class. Using the Social Capital Tracker, guide each learner into building a rich network of supportive relationships. Provide customized learning experiences for learners to lean into their advantages and receive support on areas that need development.
  - ◆ Developmental State: We're learning more and more about brain development across age ranges. Students

learn best when the learning design matches their developmental state.

- ◆ *Some tips*: Create opportunities for collaboration across age groups. Have older students mentor and coach younger students. Have younger students complete projects with older learners.

◆ Learning Differences: Kids learn best when their own unique learning differences are understood and they are given the right supports.

- ◆ *Some tips*: Allow learners to co-create learning experiences that align with their optimal mode of learning. Can learners utilize audiobooks? Graphic novels? Can they create a video instead of an essay? Can learners work at different paces? Can learners mentor each other?

The bottom line:

There are A LOT of factors that impact a person's learning. They are complex. They overlap. As education designers, our charge is to be responsive in the types of learning environments and activities we create to maximize the learning potential for young people and mitigate obstacles. Transcend's Designing for Learning framework is a great tool to have in your toolbox.

Tapping Parents, Caregivers, and Dream Teams

System Element: Community Practices and School Culture

Biggest Ripple Effect: Roles; Curriculum, Pedagogy, and Assessment; Communication

What it is and Why:

Throughout this book, we've emphasized the importance of surrounding learners with deep, caring relationships. In this chapter, as we explore how to support learners through productive struggle, it's crucial that we drive the point home. In-class and in-school experiences can help learners build habits of resilience and persistence. The impact, though, is multiplied when learners are also receiving this message at home, from parents and caregivers, and from caring adults in their lives (Dream Teams, coaches, mentors, spiritual leaders, etc.). School leaders and educators can and should tap these networks of caring adults for the benefit of the longitudinal growth of all learners. Here are some tips (many of which have already been touched on):

◆ As you admit and onboard new families, be transparent about the real challenges learners will face in a self-directed environment. It will take time for students to build the mindset and habits of guiding their own learning. It's important that families are "bought in" to this journey from the beginning.

◆ Have regular convenings for parents and caregivers. We've highlighted the technique of Parent Coffees as a way to gather the adults of the school community to have dialogue, share struggles and tips, and gain deeper understanding of the school model.

◆ Keep the learner at the center of conversations around their progress. That's not to say that leaders and educators can't or shouldn't proactively communicate to parents to share insights of a learner's progress, but the action step should always pivot back to the student themselves. Invite parents to have conversations with their child. Equip them with questions to ask (e.g., "What goals are you setting right now? How are you progressing on your goals? Is there anything you're struggling with or behind on? Do you need to adjust your goals or your approach to meeting your goals?").

◆ Be intentional about Dream Teams. Guide your learners to assemble their Dream Teams and meet with them regularly. Encourage students to invite their Dream Teams to school events.

◆ Utilize student-centered progress reporting. We've mentioned techniques like After Action Reviews and Learner-Led Conferences. Intentionally create times throughout the school year where the students themselves are updating their parents, caregivers, and Dream Teams about their yearly progress.

Motivators

System Element: Curriculum, Pedagogy, and Assessment

Biggest Ripple Effect: Roles; Communications

What it is and Why:
What motivates someone to learn? There's a lot we could say here. Many books have been written about motivating students. There are undergraduate- and graduate-level courses devoted to the subject. We're going to be brief because, in the scope of this book, motivators are a technique. They are a set of tools educators use to boost student engagement. We also believe that, collectively, the techniques throughout this book will also boost student motivation. That being said, it's still fitting for motivators to have their own space as a technique. Here's a helpful way to build a variety of motivators into each and every learning experience:

How to do it:
Think about motivators along two spectra.

The first is **intrinsic and extrinsic**. Someone who is intrinsically motivated finds the experience inherently rewarding and enjoyable. Extrinsic motivators, by contrast, are external factors that can be positive (prizes/rewards) or negative (consequences). The Industrial Age model of school design is mainly built on extrinsic motivators. Students go to school because they have to, and they do the work to get good grades and avoid bad grades. In learner-led schools, students have more opportunities to follow their curiosity and make meaningful choices in their education, which boost their intrinsic motivation. That's not to say that extrinsic motivators can't be used in self-directed learning as well. As adults, we're aware of how external factors motivate us in our personal and career goals. Likewise, extrinsic motivators can be used in school to boost a learner's attention and energy *for a short time*. Students who depend on extrinsic motivators and haven't cultivated their own internal drive will struggle as the journey gets more difficult.

The second continuum is **individual and group** motivators. Learning is deeply personal and different learners will be individually motivated by different things. By leveraging group dynamics, educators can use positive peer pressure to increase the energy and engagement in the classroom. A mixture of extrinsic and intrinsic motivators split across individuals and groups can be a powerful tool for educators. The chart below gives some examples in each category:

TABLE 9.1 Motivators

Individual (intrinsic)	Group (intrinsic)
◆ Encourage learners to follow their natural curiosity	◆ Meaningful work that helps others
◆ Guide learners to set their own learning goals	◆ Provide choice or flexibility in groupings
◆ The work is in the learner's "challenge zone"	◆ All groups to choose their resources, deliverables, and assessments
◆ Provide customization so learners can choose resources, deliverables, and how they are assessed	◆ Scaffold the work so that each group member tackles material in their "Challenge Zone"
◆ Build on prior skills and knowledge	◆ Provide ways for each member of the group to bring in their own interests
◆ Make the learning mastery-based	◆ Make the learning mastery-based
◆ Guide learners to reflect on their purpose and identify how the work is relevant	◆ Ensure each learner feels a deep sense of belonging
	◆ Cultivate camaraderie among groups by utilizing regular team-building activities

(Continued)

TABLE 9.1 (Continued)

Individual (extrinsic)	Group (extrinsic)
◆ Graduating/Advancing Levels	◆ Competitions/Prizes
◆ Competitions/Prizes	◆ Natural consequences
◆ Earned freedoms	◆ Contingent celebrations (e.g., if everyone turns in quality work by the deadline, the class gets a pizza party)
◆ Natural consequences	
◆ Public showcasing of work	◆ A chance to meet experts
	◆ Public showcasing of work

Conclusion

This chapter highlights one of the key mindset shifts made by leaders, educators, learners, and parents in self-directed environments: learning should be challenging and young people need to develop the skills, mindsets, and habits to productively struggle and persevere in their work. Again, we aren't advocating for creating high-anxiety, panic-inducing environments. Rather, we encourage leaders and educators to allow learners to experience right-sized challenges that push them out of their comfort zone. Allowing learners to experience productive struggle promotes critical thinking, resilience, and creativity while deepening their understanding of concepts. Through grappling with challenges, learners develop problem-solving skills and a growth mindset, increasing their motivation and engagement. Productive struggle fosters self-regulation and metacognitive skills, preparing learners to navigate real-world challenges with confidence. Do we want our students to become independent thinkers capable of overcoming obstacles and achieving success in academics and beyond? If so, then we must let young people endure challenges and struggle along the way as we coach, support, encourage, and guide them.

References

Borgonovi, F., & Han, S. W. (2021). Gender disparities in fear of failure among 15-year-old students: The role of gender inequality, the organization of schooling and economic conditions. *Journal of Adolescence*, *86*(1), 28–39.

Charlot, J., Leck, C., and Saxberg, B. (2020). *Designing for learning primer*. Transcend, Inc. https://transcendeducation.org/wp-content/uploads/2022/12/DesigningforLearningPrimer_Transcend_WebVersion_Feb_2020.pdf

Duckworth, A. (2016). *Grit: The power of passion and perseverance*. Simon and Schuster.

Dweck, C. (2006). *Mindset: The new psychology of success*. Random House.

Nottingham, J. (2024, May 30). The learning pit. https://www.learningpit.org

Schwartz, B. (2004). *The paradox of choice: Why less is more*. ECCO.

Thornton, M. (2023). *Classroom detracking in the US: Examples for school leadership*. Springer Press.

10

Facilitating Learner-Led Assessment

Usually, one of the first questions that comes up in a discussion about self-directed learning is assessment. For decades, assessment has ruled over education discourse. In most cases, though, it has become the tail that wags the dog. Instead of being a tool for providing students with feedback on their work, authentically measuring progress, or displaying mastery, too many assessments have become little more than numbers on paper. They don't mean anything. They don't tell a story. They're data points, often disconnected from the actual learning that is happening in any given classroom.

There is a place for assessment. For real, authentic assessment that means something to the learner being assessed. For assessment that provides a snapshot into a specific learning journey, that gives the learner an evaluation of strengths and areas for growth. We all benefit from high-quality assessments, in our learning, in our work, and in our relationships. When it comes to standardized testing, though, it's tempting to lose the narrative. We spend time talking about test scores. About high or low test

DOI: 10.4324/9781003489894-10

scores. About how to improve test scores. Less often are we talking about the tests themselves. Why do we need them? What are they measuring? Does any of it matter?

An influential study from Ruth Butler (1988) divided 5th and 6th grade learners into two groups. One group received grades with no comment on their work; the other group received constructive comments but no grades. Butler found a stark divide in the first group: students that received high grades continued to be engaged in the work, but learners that received lower grades disengaged over time. This motivation divide wasn't observed in the group that received comments. Butler called the difference in assessment "ego-involving grades" or "task-involving comments." When learners were given grades, they internalized those grades as a label for their own competencies (high-achieving learners stayed high-achieving and low-achieving learners stayed low-achieving). But when the focus was on the work itself (through "task-involving comments")—not a label on the student—learners across the spectrum of achievement stayed engaged in the learning.

As you go about cultivating self-directed learning in your own context, you'll need to think deeply about what assessment looks like. There's an old saying: you measure what you value. So, part of thinking about assessments begins with the topics from earlier chapters. What is your Portrait of a Graduate? What should be true of all the young people that graduate from your environment? What have they had intentional practice doing? How have they shown mastery?

Another key feature of assessment in learner-led spaces that is different from traditional schools: who is doing the assessing? In a learner-led space, learners will get experience being evaluated by educators and content experts. It doesn't end there, though. They will get experience receiving feedback from their peers, especially as they engage with collaborative work. They'll also build ample skills around self-evaluation. A truly self-directed learner has built the habits and mindsets to know how to judge what they know and what they don't. They can measure their work against quality exemplars and make their own plans for revision. They can pair feedback from multiple sources and synthesize an action plan. In other words, they know how to use assessment as a valuable tool. They can *learn* from assessment and look forward to assessments with a kind of excitement. They see them as learning opportunities.

That's a vastly different mindset than schools that instill deeply-rooted anxieties around test taking. Tests shouldn't be things to be feared. They should be seen as places to show what you know, so that you can get actionable feedback on the next stage of the journey.

A Story

A high school sociology teacher in Pike County, Georgia received an email from one of his students. The student asked if, instead of a final exam, they could create a final project for the course. Here's an excerpt from the email:

> My alternate assignment for the final will fall under the following standard (found in the GDOE [Georgia Department of Education]):
>
> SSSocC1 Explain the development and importance of culture.
>
> a. Describe how culture is a social construction.
> b. Identify the basic elements of culture.
> c. Explain the importance of culture as an organizing tool in society.
> d. Describe the components of culture to include language, symbols, norms, and values; also include material and non-material culture.

The student then goes on to articulate how their project—which would infuse a variety of artistic mediums—would hit every aspect of the standard.

Think of all of the competencies this learner is exemplifying. They know how to search out and find the standards for their course on the state's Department of Education website. They crafted a compelling pitch to their educator for how they could showcase mastery of the standards in a way that was interesting and motivating to them. They know how to advocate for themselves. They are not trying to "get off the hook" of assessment. Rather, they are trying to tie the assessment to a project of interest. This is a simple, yet powerful example of a learner *owning* their assessment.

Techniques

Practicals

System Element: Curriculum, Pedagogy, and Assessment

Biggest Ripple Effect: Community Practices and School Culture; Roles; Schedules

What it is and Why:
Think of how a karate student engages in a test of skill to move up in ranking. Or how firefighters demonstrate mastery by going in front of their superiors and proving, through simulations, they are ready. Practicals work in much the same way. We (as school leaders and educators) clearly define the competencies (which connect to our Portrait of a Graduate) and create single-point rubrics for each one. Then, we orient learners around the competency and give them multiple opportunities to practice and prepare. We then schedule Practicals, and learners bring a multitude of evidence (from in and out of school) to

showcase their mastery of the competency. A panel gives learners feedback on their work and gives one of two answers: Yes, mastery has been shown, or Not Yet, more work remains to be done. The evidence presented by learners becomes part of their mastery transcript.

How to do it:
Design a system of Practicals that works in your setting. Here are the twelve elements we build into our process:

1. Competency-based
2. Clear learning objectives (definitions of competencies)
3. Clear criteria for mastery (single-point rubrics)
4. Comprehensive assessment methods (eg, tests, Q&A, performance tasks, presentations) to get a holistic view
5. Self-paced
6. Opportunities for revision and feedback
7. Authentic, real-world application
8. Focus on retention and transfer
9. Comprehensive reporting and documentation
10. Continuous improvement
11. Have older learners help younger learners
12. Significant time in the schedule for orientation, preparation, participating in the practical, and reflecting on feedback

An example:
Logan County District Schools in Kentucky call these assessments Defenses of Learning. They have built in Defense of Learning experiences throughout their entire K-12 school model. The following chart shows their expectations across grade bands:

Grade Band Progression of Defense Expectations

K–3rd	4th–5th	6th–8th	9th–12th
• K-3 will continue to participate in exhibition of learning nights—these presentations can be modified as needed. • K will choose 2 competencies and collect a minimum of one piece of evidence for each of those competencies. (These can be class chosen.) • 1st will choose 2 competencies, and collect a minimum of 2 pieces per chosen competency. (This can include a class and an individual competency.) • 2nd will choose 2 competencies and have a minimum 2 pieces of individual evidence per competency. (These pieces of evidence can be combined with evidence gathered in grade 3 and be used in 3rd grade DOL presentations.) • 3rd grade will do formal defenses of learning—Focus on 2 competencies with 2 pieces of evidence for each competency addressed.	• 4-5 will continue to participate in exhibition of learning nights—exhibition presentations should incorporate profile competency language. ("When I worked on this project, I was an innovator because...") • 4th grade will continue to collect evidence for each profile competency that can be combined with 5th grade evidence for the 5th-grade DOL presentation. • 5th grade will do formal defenses of learning—Focus on 3 competencies—2 they felt successful in and 1 they need to work on improving.	• 6-8 will present to their parents regarding their profile growth at student-led conferences. • 8th grade will use their student-led conference as practice for their formal panel defense. • 6-8 will collect evidence that can be used to support growth in all 5 competencies. Students can use evidence gathered during any of their middle school years to support their formal defense in 8th grade. • 8th grade will do formal defenses of learning—Focus on 4 competencies—3 they felt successful in and 1 they need to improve.	• Successfully completing a formal defense that addresses all 5 competencies of the Profile of Success by the end of 12th grade is a graduation requirement. • 9-12 grades will collect evidence related to each competency that can be used towards any of their defense presentations. • All grades (9-12) will do Defense of Learning presentations regarding their profile growth. The audiences will vary each year, but will progress from groups of teachers and peers to formal panels for 12th grade. (High School has specific protocols for this.)

FIGURE 10.1 Logan County Schools Grade Band Progression of Defense Expectations (Logan County Profile of Success, 2024).

Like Practicals, these defenses are tied to the district's Profile of a Graduate, are learner-led, and are mastery-based (as exemplified by the evidence that learners collect and present).

World-Class Examples

System Element: Curriculum, Pedagogy, and Assessment

Biggest Ripple Effect: Tech and Tech Infrastructure

What it is and Why:
In every field, industry, and artform there are "master" examples. A world-class example is just that: *a real model of the "thing" in the world done well*. This can apply to any task and assignment a student is undertaking. A book report? Here are some examples of high-quality published critiques. A presentation? Here are a few TED Talks to watch for inspiration. Creative writing? Here's a diverse list of great short stories. The value of a world-class example isn't just that it provides a great role model; it's that it provides learners a way to assess their own work. When we compare our work to that of a master, we can see the gap. We can identify the strengths and weaknesses of our work. We can make a plan to get better.

How to do it:
1. Every time you give an assignment to students, provide world-class examples. If you can't find a good example, it means the work you're asking students to do doesn't carry over to the real world. And if it doesn't carry over to the real world, then you might want to consider if it's an assignment worth giving.
2. Provide diverse examples. Showcase quality work from a variety of cultures and viewpoints.
3. Generate your own list of exemplars. Get your team to add to it. Tap your network. Get community input.

4. Guide learners to find and identify world-class examples. Discovering, vetting, and critiquing masterworks is a great skill to build.

5. Prompt reflection. Give students a list of questions to consider as they study an example. Some possible questions:
   1. What do you notice about this example?
   2. What does this work do well? How could this work be improved?
   3. What elements of this work could you imitate or replicate right now?
   4. How does this work compare to your own? What are the major differences you notice between your work and the example? How large is the "gap" between the quality of this work and your own? What skills do you need to practice or what knowledge do you need to gain in order to close that gap? What resources do you need access to? How confident are you that, given the right resources and time to practice, you could produce a work that's close to the example?

6. Cultivate a growth-mindset culture. Showing world-class examples doesn't mean that we're setting an impossibly high bar for our learners to clear. It means we're showing them types of work they can move toward with the right combination of discipline, practice, and talent.

Learner-created Rubrics

System Element: Curriculum, Pedagogy, and Assessment

Biggest Ripple Effect: Roles; Community Practices

What it is and Why:
Creating rubrics is a skill that all teachers build. It's important to clearly define the parameters and expectations of deliverables we give students and rubrics provide clarity and transparency in the

assessment process. Making rubrics is usually within the locus of control of a classroom teacher. While many things may seem out of their hands (curriculum, pacing, standards, etc.), most teachers have full autonomy in creating rubrics. This is a great way to pivot toward greater student agency! What if you supported and encouraged learners at your school to design their own rubrics? What sort of skills and mindsets might that cultivate? How might that impact their engagement with the assignment? The simple act of creating a rubric is loaded with learning opportunities that deepens learners' understanding of the material and boosts their own sense of autonomy.

How to do it:

1. Make it clear to learners what is and isn't in their locus of control. Is there a set deadline? Is there a required modality? What are the elements they must include in their rubric?
2. Provide world-class examples. Find (or create) rubrics that learners can see and use as templates.
3. Make it iterative. Find ways to give learners feedback on their rubrics and have them revise and resubmit.
4. Honor the rubric they create. Have that be the metric used in their assessment.
5. Invite reflection. After the project, have learners reflect on the quality of their rubric. Was it an authentic assessment of their work? Did it provide meaningful feedback? If they were to create the rubric again, what would they do differently?

Expert Evaluations

System Element: Roles

Biggest Ripple Effect: Bridges and Partnerships; Curriculum, Pedagogy, and Assessment

What it is and Why:
Teachers are more and more treated like unicorns. They're expected to be world-class managers, deeply-knowledgeable content experts, top-notch relationship builders, and masters of assessment. One of the key ways teachers can transition to a more guide/coach/facilitator mode is to redirect where evaluation is coming from. What if, instead of educators always acting in the role of evaluator, feedback came from experts out in the field? Making this pivot opens up some exciting possibilities: (1) it adds authenticity to the assignment by connecting to real-world industry, (2) it allows the educator to fully function as guide and coach (not evaluator), (3) it *frees up* time the educator would otherwise spend on grading/assessing, and (4) it allows for richer feedback.

How to do it:
- **Tap your network**: A key role of the school leader in this is to be actively building your own network and lending your social capital to your team. A re-imagined role of an educator in a leader-led environment is someone who is expanding and utilizing their own network while helping learners build theirs. Make inroads within your community and don't be afraid to ask for expertise when you need it.
- **Utilize parents and caregivers**: Within your school community are a wide array of parents and caregivers who are experts in their fields. As part of your relationship building, get to know the work your parents are doing and invite them into school to share their expertise.
- **Give a clear ask**: When inviting outside experts, clearly articulate what you'd like them to do. Are they reviewing prototypes? Are they watching demonstrations? Provide them with the deliverables, rubrics, and expectations ahead of time.

- **Take advantage of technology**: We're in an age where you can have an expert from anywhere in the world video conference with your students.
- **Invite real-world feedback**: This isn't a "career day" type of activity. You're not asking these experts just to come in and talk about their jobs. They're coming in to give learners honest feedback about the strengths and weaknesses of their work. Invite experts to bring the thunder! Have them give honest assessments to learners. This is a great opportunity for learners to gain guidance on how they can deepen their knowledge and sharpen their skills in a specific topic.
- **Give learners the opportunity to reflect**: It's tempting to see a moment of evaluation as the "end" of a learning project. We're firm believers that the most important learning happens next, after learners have received robust feedback from peers, educators, and experts. Create time and space for learners to reflect on the feedback they received and make sense of it. This can happen in whole groups, small groups, and individually.

Developing Quality Peer Feedback

System Element: Curriculum, Pedagogy, and Assessment

Biggest Ripple Effect: Roles

What it is and Why:
Giving high-quality feedback to a classroom of 30+ students is a challenge most teachers face. One way to reframe the challenge: envision all the students in your class not only as *recipients* of feedback, but also as *givers* of high-quality assessment. Research has shown that peer feedback is more effective in increasing student performance than strictly teacher evaluation (Sackstein, 2017). That being said, learners need practice, protocols, and

preparation as they grow in their ability to give quality feedback. Here are some ideas to get started.

How to do it:

- ◆ Guiding questions. Create a simple list of questions that students can ask each other to prompt deeper thinking and reflection of their work. Sample questions could be:
  - ◆ Have you done work like this before? If so, do you think you did better work this time than last time?
  - ◆ Have you compared your work to a world-class example? What do you think are the current strengths and weaknesses of your work?
  - ◆ If you had to do this assignment over again, what's one thing you would change about your process?
  - ◆ If you had a chance to revise your work, what's one major change you would make?
- ◆ Provide a rubric. Have learners assess their peers according to the rubric that was given with the assignment.
- ◆ Feedback protocols. Equip learners with a process for giving feedback. Some examples:
  - ◆ *"I like...I wish...I wonder..."* Ask learners to give feedback with something they liked about the work, something they wish was different (or noticed was lacking) in the work, and a provocation for further reflection (e.g., "What if you tried....?).
  - ◆ *Glows and Grows.* Have learners identify two things that are strengths of the world and two things that could be improved.
- ◆ Critique groups. Organize regular, low-stakes work groups for learners to share works-in-progress and receive feedback. For these to work well, the classroom culture needs to be one that embraces a growth mindset, process-oriented approach to work.

♦ Share outs. For every assignment, create a way for learners to share their work with their peers. Depending on time constraints and class size, it may not be possible to share in a whole-group setting. Students could be divided into small groups or pairs, or "post" their work in the classroom and participate in a gallery walk, where they take turns looking over each other's work and leaving feedback (Post-it notes work well for this).

♦ Competitions. Create public value for students' work by having them vote on the best example of work and awarding some prize or honor.

An example:
Northern Cass School District in North Dakota created a peer-review process called Luminaries. Luminaries is a voluntary group of high school juniors and seniors that receive training in how to give other learners quality feedback. The Luminaries take turns being scheduled in the library and students from any class can sign up for mentoring or feedback sessions. In return, Luminary members are given course credit for mentorship.

Embracing Iterations (Perpetual Beta)
System Element: Curriculum, Pedagogy, and Assessment

Biggest Ripple Effect: Roles; Communications

What it is and Why:
There's a saying in martial arts: "progress, not perfection." Most academic-related performance metrics are focused on end results (test scores, GPAs, etc.). Less celebrated (or even acknowledged) is the growth that happens in a learning journey. What if a class culture was *more* focused on a learner's improvement over the course of a learning project than it was on the final product? How might that change the mindsets and attitudes of the learners? In

the business world, this is called "perpetual beta." The term, borrowed from software engineering, focuses on iteration and improvement. The underlying idea is that we can always get better from one iteration to the next. So, how does perpetual beta work in the classroom? Here are some ideas.

How it works:
- ◆ Break every deliverable into drafts. Instead of expecting learners to turn in a polished final product, have them turn in a rough draft and get feedback. Then have them revise into a second draft and perhaps a third or fourth. Build in iterations, feedback loops, reflection protocols, and celebrate the growth that happens each step of the way.
- ◆ Measure growth. If all learners are evaluated on is a final product, then it gives the message that meaningful improvement across iterations isn't valuable. What if we also measured growth between iterations?
- ◆ Highlight protocols in business and art. The process of iteration is closely aligned with how we work in the real world. We create drafts. We get feedback from colleagues and supervisors. We tweak and revise. So, when you give an assignment to students, highlight (or better yet, bring in an external expert to highlight) how similar work would be done in a real setting.
- ◆ Embrace failure. Most students are terrified to make mistakes, take risks, and be penalized (and shamed) for getting something wrong. Create a culture that celebrates failure and that sees mistakes as stepping stones for deep learning.

Make Learning Public
System Element: Curriculum, Pedagogy, and Assessment

Biggest Ripple Effect: Roles

What it is and Why:

Think of a student in your school. What percentage of their work makes it beyond the teacher's desk? Students are very perceptive about the "value" assigned to their work. They know when it's busy work. They know when it's just for a grade. On the flip side, they know when there's real relevance to it. Imagine these two scenarios: "Student A" is tasked with writing a book report that will be graded by a teacher; "Student B" is tasked with recording a podcast episode critiquing the same book and sharing it widely with a public audience. Which student will be more motivated to make sure their work is top-notch? Adding public value to a learner's work does four things: (1) higher visibility/scrutiny encourages the student to take their work more seriously, (2) "publishing" the work publicly adds relevance to the work (real people publish book reviews, podcast episodes, or TikTok critiques), (3) knowing other people will see and experience their work increases the energy/motivation of the class as a group, and (4) people that see the work can offer additional feedback to the learner.

How to do it:

- ◆ Have an external audience for every major assignment you give your students.
- ◆ Host student-led "public exhibitions" at the culmination of a unit or project. Having learners present their work publicly is a great way to move from a culture of completion (finishing assignments for a grade) to a culture of mastery (being able to publicly demonstrate competence).
- ◆ Invite the public audience to share feedback. This can be a simple form (online or physical) where attendees of the public exhibition can highlight the strengths of the public demonstration as well as feedback for how it could be improved.
- ◆ Create class time after the public exhibition for learners to see and make sense of their feedback, reflect on the experience, and plan for the future.

360 Feedback

System Element: Curriculum, Pedagogy, and Assessment

Biggest Ripple Effect: Continuous Learning and Improvement Mechanisms; Roles; Tech and Tech Infrastructure

What it is and Why:

In the corporate world, 360 feedback is a multi-tiered evaluative tool where an employee receives feedback from their peers. Instead of only "top-down" evaluations from management, 360 feedback provides a larger sampling of how someone is showing up to work and being experienced by their coworkers. Similarly, employing 360 feedback in a classroom is a technique for allowing learners to give each other feedback (instead of the teacher being the sole evaluator).

How to do it:

- Create a process for anonymized feedback (this can be done using Google Forms).
- Create a list of questions that can be assessed quantitatively. For example, "On a scale from 1 to 10, how would you rate this student's ability to collaborate with others?"
- Create space for qualitative feedback. For example, "What's one way this student is positively impacting the class culture?"
- Curate the data before you share it out. Students are growing in their ability to give each other quality feedback. As such, filter out unhelpful (as well as rude/hurtful) comments.
- Share the data out with learners and build time in the schedule for them to read the data, make meaning out of it, and reflect on what goals they want to set. For example, if I scored low on collaboration, I might create a strategy around how to be a better collaborator in the future.

Conclusion

How can we shift assessment practices in schools to be more learner-centered? How can we cultivate inclusive learning environments that prioritizes student growth and development? The techniques in this chapter are useful tools, but their impact will be multiplied if the techniques are part of a greater shift in how schools assess. Here are some large pivots that schools can make:

> **More formative, less summative assessment.** Incorporating formative assessment strategies that focus on providing ongoing feedback and support to students throughout their learning journey. Rather than solely relying on summative assessments at the end of a unit or term, formative assessments allow teachers to gauge students' understanding in real time, identify areas for improvement, and tailor instruction to meet individual needs. By actively involving students in the assessment process and encouraging self-reflection, formative assessments empower learners to take ownership of their learning and track their progress over time. As Tom Klapp at Northern Cass School District in North Dakota put it: "We prioritize the process over the product. As students create their final deliverables, we are providing assessments throughout the process to evaluate their learning and their growth—not just evaluating the thing they turn in."
>
> **Embracing authentic assessment methods that align with real-world tasks and challenges.** Authentic assessments provide students with opportunities to apply their knowledge and skills in meaningful contexts, such as project-based learning, simulations, or performance tasks. By engaging students in tasks that mirror authentic, real-world experiences, these assessments not only assess students' understanding but also promote critical thinking, problem-solving, and collaboration skills. Moreover,

authentic assessments allow for greater flexibility and creativity in demonstrating mastery, accommodating diverse learning styles and interests while fostering a deeper understanding of the subject matter.

Promoting a culture of growth mindset within schools can further enhance learner-centered assessment practices. Emphasizing the value of effort, resilience, and continuous improvement, a growth mindset approach encourages students to view challenges as opportunities for learning and growth rather than obstacles to be avoided. By reframing mistakes and failures as valuable learning experiences, teachers can create a supportive environment where students feel safe to take risks, explore new ideas, and embrace productive struggle. By fostering a growth mindset among students, assessment in schools can become more learner-centered, focusing not only on measuring achievement but also on nurturing the skills, attitudes, and dispositions essential for lifelong learning and success.

References

Butler, R. (1988). Enhancing and undermining intrinsic motivation: The effects of task-involving and ego-involving evaluation on interest and performance. *British Journal of Educational Psychology*, *58*(1), 1–14.

Logan County Profile of Success - K-12 resources. (2024, May 30). https://sites.google.com/logan.kyschools.us/lc-innovator-examples/k-12-resources?authuser=0

Sackstein, S. (2017). *Peer feedback in the classroom: Empowering students to be the experts*. ASCD.

11

Designing a Learner-Led Environment

The design of a space says a lot about the purpose of a space. Why are traditional school environments designed the way they are? Foucault (1995), after a lengthy exploration of how society had embraced surveillance and control of citizens, offered this critical observation: "Is it surprising that prisons resemble factories, schools, barracks, hospitals, which all resemble prisons?" (p. 228). Schools, like prisons and factories, are institutions designed to control. How would an environment that fosters freedom differ in design?

What are the things that comprise a learning environment? There are lots of considerations. The location and architecture of the building. The management of space. Interior decoration and design, the type and layout of the furniture—all of these are *environmental* factors. Each of these design elements tells a story. Each communicates a message. And children are pretty good at deciphering the unspoken messages sent by their environments.

Let's start with a simple reflection. Imagine a classroom. Take a second to really *see it* in your mind. What furniture is in the room? How is it arranged? What story does the environment

DOI: 10.4324/9781003489894-11

tell? Many of us went to schools with separate classrooms, usually constructed with cinderblock walls. Maybe there were blackboards on the walls. The desks were fixed in rows and all faced the same direction. The teacher was usually positioned at the front, sometimes at a large desk of their own, and from their position at the front of the room they lectured.

Everything in this layout tells a story. The teacher is seen as the authority and the content knowledge expert. Learning is depicted as *listening*, maybe *reading* along in a textbook, or *taking notes* while the teacher lectured. Learning is a passive process. The knowledge is slowly and methodically transferred from the knowledge-holder (the teacher and textbook) to the knowledge-receiver (the students).

We know that this is not how deep learning works. Sure, facts can be transmitted through lectures and texts. But filing away facts is a small piece of learning. Learning is an active process. It's collaborative. It can be noisy. It can be messy. Sometimes, learning might look like chaos. Sometimes it might look like play.

The environment sets the stage. John Dewey saw the environment as the first teacher. Maria Montessori made the environment a critical piece of her pedagogy, eschewing large, immovable desks in favor of moveable, child-sized furniture. She also placed all the resources children needed at their level. This is nothing new, nothing innovative. But attending to the learning environment takes intentionality. There needs to be a *why* in every aspect of a learning space. Below are some techniques leaders can use to design and cultivate learner-centered environments.

A Story

In January 2024, we opened the new campus of The Forest School. When we started the design process, years ago, we brought our learners into the conversation. They tackled a unit of architecture and interior design. They engaged with resources and world-class examples. They interviewed experts, worked in teams to design prototypes of our future school building, received iterative feedback, and presented their final products in a public showcase. Our building now has the fingerprints of our learners all over its design.

In an article for *Getting Smart*, Danish Kurani (2024) argued that the "environment is not neutral. Our spaces influence how we feel, from moment to moment, week to week, and year to year." Given that the physical environment is not a neutral element in a child's education, what role is it playing in your school? Is your design reinforcing the idea that school is a place of little choice or freedom? Or, is the layout of your learning environment sending the clear message that this is a place designed with learners in mind, a place where they can explore, create, and collaborate as they learn?

Techniques

Managing Space (and Promoting Cross-disciplinary Uses)
What it is and Why:
Many classrooms have looked the same for much of the past century. Rows of desks, facing forward. A teacher, standing or sitting at the front of the room. The simple layout of space communicates a lot about the learning environment. When setting up a classroom, here are a few questions to consider:

♦ Where are learners focusing their attention and why?
♦ How is collaboration encouraged and made possible?
♦ What type of work is this setup conducive for?
♦ What is posted on the walls?
♦ What resources are available? Where are they placed? When and to whom are they available?

There are a lot of constraints educators face when it comes to class layout: tight budgets, large class sizes, minimal time to rearrange between classes, and furniture decisions that are out of the hands of most classroom teachers. We believe simple tweaks can move any classroom toward a more learner-centered environment.

How to do it:

Design your classroom for multimodal learning. Consider the following modalities:

- ◆ *Discussion*: Is your classroom layout conducive to group discussions? Some tips: arrange seating in the shape of a circle (or u-shape) so that learners can face each other in discussions.

- ◆ *Exploration*: Is your classroom layout conducive to learners to get into "flow states" during work? There are a variety of examples out there (trendy co-working spaces, cool coffee shops, modern libraries, workspaces at tech companies, etc.) that show how interior design (lighting, decor, furniture arrangement, acoustics) boost individual focus and attention. Again, you can only control what you can control, but consider how your classroom layout can inspire and empower learners to do their own exploration, research, and work.

- ◆ *Making*: Is your classroom layout conducive to hands-on exploration? Some schools have dedicated "maker spaces" where learners can tinker. Every classroom, though, can be designed to incorporate "making" into the learning environment. Have a designated space in your classroom for resources and materials and create a protocol that clarifies expectations on when and how learners engage with materials.

- ◆ *Sharing*: Is your classroom layout conducive to learners sharing their work? This could come via presentations in whole or small groups, or exhibit-style gallery walks. The mode of the "share out" will influence the class layout (and vice versa).

In addition to these modalities, your class can fluctuate to incorporate individual and group work. We'll discuss this more in the following techniques.

Interior Design

System Element: Facilities

Biggest Ripple Effect: Budget; Roles

What it is and Why:
We agree with Danish Kurani that space is not neutral. The aesthetics of a space have a real impact on the moods, attitudes, and culture of learning in a school. That being the case, school leaders have a responsibility to oversee the creation of intentionally beautiful spaces. Again, we know the constraints: budgets, buy-in from other leaders or board members, building codes, etc. These are real limitations. Our argument, though, is that the architecture and interior design of a learning environment is a crucial element to learning design. Drab, industrial buildings will continue to cultivate drab, industrial school design.

How to do it:
This isn't so much of a "how-to." Rather, as a leader, connect your vision and mission for the school to the aesthetics of the space. Make this a key part of your pitch when you talk to district- and state-level leaders, board members, funders, and community members. Create a compelling pitch about what your school would look and feel like. Danish Kurani has great resources for school leaders considering architecture and design on his website (https://kurani.us).

Furniture for Flow

What it is and Why:
The choice of classroom furniture is usually out of the hands of most teachers. When considering furniture decisions, though,

decision-makers should choose furniture that encourages learners to get into flow and focus on their work. Here are things to consider:

+ *Comfort*: Students spend a lot of time in class furniture, so make it comfortable! A way to increase the focused attention of your learners is to ensure that they're not taken out of flow by uncomfortable seating.
+ *Durability*: Kids can be hard on furniture. One of the reasons school seats and desks are so rigid is that the furniture built for the Industrial Age of schooling was built to last. With new advancements in material and manufacturing, school furniture can be durable *and* comfortable.
+ *Flexibility*: More and more schools are utilizing "flex" furniture that can easily adjust to different class configurations. This type of furniture allows for independent solo focus, can adapt into small clusters for group work and collaboration, and can move around easily between discussions and work time.
+ *Variety*: Differentiating spaces in the classroom for different types of work can create a cohesive, yet dynamic space. Some classes have reading nooks, focus zones, collaboration stations, and maker spaces.

Choice in Seating

What it is and Why:

We've discussed student choice in a variety of places throughout the book. Here, we'll highlight how the environment itself lends itself to boosting learner agency. As we've already discussed in this chapter, the look, feel, and overall design of a classroom says a lot about what kinds of work happen in a space. So, as you attend to the physical design of the space, be intentional about increasing *the choices learners can make* within that space.

Some ideas:

- ♦ Have a graduated approach where learners can earn more and more freedom to choose their seating.
- ♦ Play with the schedule. Maybe there are certain days/ times when learners have more choice in seating?

Get Outdoors

What it is and Why:

This is not so much a technique as it is an encouragement. We recognize that not all schools are going to have access to nature and that encouraging educators to get their learners "outdoors" is a recommendation loaded with privilege. That being said, there's a lot of research on human flourishing that points to the educative power of being outside in nature (Weir, 2020). Kids spend a lot of their time at school. The majority of that time is spent sitting at desks and an increasing percentage of that time is spent looking at screens. As we discuss the environment of learning, we'd be remiss for not mentioning the role that natural environments play in childhood development. That's not to say that schools bear all the responsibility for providing young people experience in nature (as school age students only spend about 18% of their waking hours at school). Parents have a role in encouraging and opting into outdoor experiences. Communities have a role in providing green spaces. Young people may choose to do afterschool sports or activities that are predominantly outside. But as we think about the design of school broadly and the school environment specifically, we should be aware of the importance of getting kids outside.

Here are some ideas and wonderings:

- ♦ Utilize the outdoor space your school provides. How often can you tap into your current resources? Is having class outside an option? If so, how can you maximize your outside space while still working toward your learning objectives and standards?

◆ Cultivate community connections. Is there a park nearby? How can your school become users and caretakers of the greenspace?

◆ Build partnerships. What organizations in your community are committed to outdoor education and environmental stewardship? In what ways you can partner with these organizations to provide your learners with access to natural environments and meaningful learning experiences?

◆ Field Trips. There are a number of competing field trip destinations in a school year. As you plan out of school excursions for your students, consider how a field trip could provide your learners an experience in nature.

Class Cleaning/Organizing

System Element: Roles; Facilities

Biggest Ripple Effect: Community Practices and School Culture; Communications

What it is and Why:
How many students see their classrooms as something they have a sense of responsibility over? One technique for building a positive class culture is creating a sense of shared ownership over the space itself. What if learners were the ones who ensured the floors were swept, the chairs were stacked, and the supplies were organized? This isn't an easy technique. It's often easier for us adults to do this work ourselves. But, if done consistently, expecting learners to be the caretakers of the classroom and holding them accountable for doing so builds in a collective responsibility.

How to do it:

♦ Create a list of "jobs to be done" and a system for getting the work done, be it assigned jobs (e.g., a learner is assigned to take out the trash) or assigned spaces (e.g., the class area is divided up between teams).

♦ Publicly celebrate learners who do top-notch work.

♦ Have a system of accountability for learners who do not do their jobs.

♦ Create incentives for outstanding class cleanliness and organization and consider including competitions.

♦ "Hold up a mirror" at the end of the day or the beginning of the next day and invite learners to rate and reflect on the cleanliness of the classroom.

Conclusion

What are the things that comprise a learning environment? There are lots of considerations. The location and architecture of the building. The management of space. Interior decoration and design, the type and layout of the furniture—all of these are *environmental* factors. So, arguably the first part of setting up an environment for learner-led education is to intentionally design the space. Pay attention to the aesthetic factors. Pay attention to the emotive power that simple choices like the layout of furniture or the color of paint can have. In what ways can schools, in their architecture and design, more resemble places of comfort, safety, and belonging? It is no coincidence that many of the self-directed theorists of the last century have modeled their learning spaces on the idea of *home* (Maria Montessori named her school Casa Bambini, or Children's Home). In designing with the learner in mind, take intentional care to move away from the institutional/ factory/prison aesthetic and more toward a space that is welcoming, comforting, and nurturing.

References

Foucault, M. (1995). *Discipline and punish: The birth of the prison*. Vintage Books.

Kurani, D. (2024, May 7). How to design a school for Belonging. Getting Smart. https://www.gettingsmart.com/2024/04/18/how-to-design-a-school-for-belonging/

Weir, K. (2020, April 1). Nurtured by nature. https://www.apa.org. https://www.apa.org/monitor/2020/04/nurtured-nature

12

Leading School Transformation

This book, with its techniques and tips, is meant to be an addition to the school leader's toolkit. But it's not *just* that. It's an argument. An invitation. A call to action. The outdated Industrial Model of education isn't serving learners in the present and it sure isn't setting them up for success in the future. To truly help our students thrive, we need to equip them to be agile learners, able to adapt, to learn and re-learn to an ever-changing world. With that in mind, let's briefly step back, consider what brought us to this point, and highlight how we as school leaders can build better schools.

The Achievement Era in Hindsight

We haven't arrived at our current state haphazardly. In her book *Schooling America*, former Harvard Graduate School of Education dean Patricia Graham (2005) divides a century's worth of educational history into four distinct eras, which she labels as the

DOI: 10.4324/9781003489894-12

four A's: Assimilation, Adjustment, Access, and Achievement. We've been in the latter focus of Achievement, she contends, since the 1980s and the publication of *A Nation At Risk* (National Commission on Excellence in Education, 1983). The focus in this phase has been on shepherding students toward academic achievement and gainful employment. We've stiffened school structures to hit this bullseye.

Five-ish decades in, the Achievement Era has been a mixed bag. Some upsides of an achievement focus are increased accountability, measurable progress, and student preparation for success (in some arenas). But there are plenty of downsides, including an overemphasis on grades, fear of failure, a sense of competition over collaboration, and an overreliance on adults for both instruction and validation. With an achievement focus, students are incentivized to seek satisfaction and assess their self-worth through accomplishment and others' opinions.

The most insidious downside of the Achievement epoch is that all students are guided to learn the same or similar skills, knowledge, and mindsets (i.e., one size fits all) instead of being guided toward their own personal growth. When children are pushed to achieve goals that are set by others, they lack self-direction. That is a tragedy. Like adults, every young person has thoughts, feelings, and plans. Unfortunately, the design of the Industrial-Age school model—a batch-processing approach—usually shuts them down in children. People become dependent when they lack awareness of their thoughts, feelings, and plans.

But what if the opposite were true? What if schools empowered children to flourish? What if schools were the places where they could explore, identify, express, and develop their thoughts, feelings, and goals? There's power in the uniqueness of every child. It's time that school designs honor students' unique calling, preferences, and goals, and encourage them to pursue those. It's time to move fully into a new era for learning where learners can develop greater self-leadership than ever before.

Building a Future-Ready System

Thankfully, the work of building a future-ready system full of excellent schools is already underway. Many leaders in the public and private school sectors are redesigning learning models to help children learn what they need in order to live the lives they want. Though their styles vary, these leaders are generally making five key moves when leading school transformation.

Articulate a bold new vision. School leaders work directly with their communities to unearth parents' and caregivers' hopes and dreams for their kids. They also ask students about their goals and treat those goals as precious and foundational. Then they co-create and champion a compelling vision for excellence in education. This vision serves as a guiding light, aligning the efforts of everyone involved. Leaders identify innovative teaching methods that foster deep disciplinary learning, student collaboration, and authentic assignments. They build new signature learning experiences that give students choice and voice. The ninja move that most leaders make at this stage is creating a vision that works within the constraints of their system. Select leaders manage to upend and reshape the landscape to improve conditions more quickly. Either way, the new vision, methods, and experiences set the stage for transformative change.

Clarify the knowledge, skills, and craft that teachers need to bring the new vision to life. With new methods, often the educator competencies required are new, too. In their preparation or prior experience, teachers may not have encountered the abilities or mindsets needed to activate new methods. Some leaders use the title "Portrait of a Teacher" to describe needed competencies. Each portrait can be tailored to the school's unique approach and serve as a framework, guiding teacher development, recruitment, and support.

Leaders design signature learning experiences for educators. Seeing themselves as learning designers, leaders create experiences that align with their vision and Portrait of a Teacher. These experiences become invaluable tools for professional development. They help ensure that what happens in classrooms matches the school's bigger vision to maximize opportunities for children. Some of this work is threading through to our nation's graduate schools of education, albeit slowly. Forward-thinking leaders start their own teacher training programs.

Leaders work tirelessly to gain buy-in for the new vision. Though the work of getting legitimacy and support starts at the first stage of co-creating a new shared vision, it is work that never ends. Change always faces resistance. So leaders must perpetually cultivate buy-in from teachers, parents, students, and school partners. Leaders find strategies to foster a deep belief in the importance of transformation. Leaders learn both public-facing and also behind-the-scenes tactics to garner support. It's incredibly hard work. It's like tilling rocky soil for a seed to take root and grow.

Leaders establish systems for continuous improvement. Amy Edmonson (2012) calls this "organizing to execute" and "organizing to learn." Transformative work is messy. No one gets it right the first time. Leaders in 'advanced player mode' figure out how to deliver quality experiences, learn quickly from imperfections, and keep the entire community informed and talking. Sustained progress amidst organizational change requires effective systems and structures. So, these leaders develop community practices, communication strategies, and continuous learning mechanisms to know what to keep doing, what to stop doing, and what to change.

Preparation is key. Leaders looking to take their schools on a transformation journey are well served by building their own leadership skills in certain areas. Particularly, racial and cultural fluency, creative problem-solving, communication, teamwork, team building, and project management are key skills that empower leaders to be top-notch guides shepherding the process.

Despite the arduous transformation journey, skilled leaders can guide communities to a promising frontier. Recalling Graham's four eras—Assimilation, Adjustment, Access, and Achievement—what if the next era in education was *Abounding*, where all students flourish? Where they can experience personal growth and opportunity. Where ultimately they're self-directed, interdependent learners instead of dependent ones. Where they can explore, express, and develop their own thoughts, feelings, and plans in service of finding a calling that will change the world. It won't be perfect, and there will be downsides. But it will be better suited for our times.

Courageous school leadership can help make this vision a reality. Let's applaud and support visionary educators helping shape our children's future. In fact, the next time you see or meet one of them, give them a hug, a high five, or an encouraging word because this work is far from easy. And it's vital for the next generation.

The Educator's Oath

In 1948, the World Medical Association (WMA) convened in Geneva and created "The Physician's Pledge" (WMA, 1948). A central tenet of the pledge signed by medical professionals is to "respect the autonomy and dignity of my patient." So, in the medical field, the right of individual autonomy has long been recognized and protected. Can we say the same about education?

It's time that we as educators ("we" in the broadest sense: school leaders, teachers, administrators, policymakers, and researchers across public, private, and charter networks) commit to a view of schooling that recognizes and respects the autonomy of the learner. This is mainly a book of "hows," techniques that any school leader or educator can use (if even in small ways) to open space in their schools for learner choice. Here, at the end of the book, we wanted to come back to *why*.

Here's a quote a partner school shared with us from a recent student survey (the respondent is a high school junior):

> At this point, a lot of things are too late for me to do. Like being able to take certain art courses. I've never really been able to express my talents or creativity in my schooling. Without my art, I have found learning difficult. I would like to have a choice in how I learn. I would like more projects and collaborative classes. I would like to have the opportunity to get closer with peers and be able to work with them and just have a solid understanding of what is going on in my education. I've just become lost in it all and I need a damn break. Sorry for my language, but everything is just so stressful and I feel like I've been blocked from doing the things I love.

We all have thoughts, interests, and curiosities. School can be a place that breathes life into those things, gives young people a safe place to learn and grow and develop. Sadly, though, a common experience of many learners is that school extinguishes their curiosity, makes no room for their interests, and doesn't ask for their thoughts or ideas.

Navigating a Choice-Filled World

Throughout this book, we have highlighted tips and techniques to boost self-directed learning in any setting. We have also presented a lot of reasons why we need such an approach to education.

We've argued that it's crucial for society. We need to cultivate generations of independent problem-solvers ready to take on the challenges of today and tomorrow. We need collaborative learners who have practiced self-governance and know how to live and learn across lines of difference. We need agile, adaptable learners that can teach themselves anything.

We've argued that it's crucial for learners. Self-directed learning cultivates resilience, emotional intelligence, cross-cultural adaptability, and overall life satisfaction. Students that get regular practice at setting and working toward their own learning goals are better positioned to identify and lean into their own sense of purpose.

We've argued that it's crucial for schools. The Industrial Age model of education is outdated. It's getting harder and harder to motivate students to attend and engage with school. Teacher burnout is on the rise. Technological advances like AI will continue to disrupt the way we do education. School leaders are recognizing they need to prioritize learner autonomy to keep education relevant and purposeful.

There are many *whys* to move toward self-directed learning. Our strong belief is that children need *freedom to make choices* in the present so they can further develop their *freedom to choose* in the future. As it stands, the Industrial Age model offers very little choice to learners. They don't have much of a say in how or what they learn. Then, we expect them to enter college or the workplace with the ability to be independent and make wise decisions. The results? College students that need a lot of hand holding. Workers that are not agile and adaptable. A spike of anxiety across the board as young people try to navigate a choice-filled world with little or no experience at making meaningful decisions in their lives.

There are schools around the world deciding on a different path. Leaders and educators across public, private, and charter school networks are making it a priority to cultivate self-directed learners. They're building it into their Profiles of a Graduate. They're making it a key pillar of their learning model. They're coaching and guiding their educators to create learner-led experiences. They're engaging with parents/caregivers, school board members, and policymakers to align on a student-centered approach. They're giving learners increased responsibility to steer their own education.

Leading school transformation is hard work, and you will get pushback from all directions. One district leader told us their first step was to get parent buy-in. They hosted community meetings. They asked parents, "What do you want for your children?" None of the responses mentioned high achievement in academics. Parents wanted their kids to be happy. To thrive. To be people of character that could choose their own futures. "That was crucial," the leader said, "it bought us time." District leaders were able to get buy-in from parents to make dramatic changes to the school system. It took a long time for the work to bear fruit. The leader went on:

> There was trepidation at first. Sure. But then, we had a high school senior who was about to fail. He wouldn't write anything. Didn't complete his assignments. When we gave him choices in his projects, he flourished. He ended up writing and publishing a book before he graduated. Turns out, his mother was a school board member. So, she became one of our biggest advocates. Eventually, test scores started rising too. Now, when people are nervous about a self-directed approach, we have tons of stories and data to point them to. It was a scary leap to make, but it was worth it.

Taking the first steps in a new direction is scary. We hope that this book has better prepared you for this work. It's meant to be a starting place. The techniques in these chapters are helpful tools in your toolbox as you seek to cultivate self-directed learning. But they are insufficient on their own. The road ahead is difficult. The obstacles are many. The temptation to stick to the status quo is great. It's possible, though, to do something different. Many courageous school leaders and educators are doing it. Our encouragement to you is to jump in and make a difference. It could be as small as working in one classroom to open up more choices for learners. It could be as large as pivoting a whole school district towards student agency. Every effort matters.

Our vocation as educators is unique. On one hand, we are focused on helping learners in the present. Meeting them where they are. Helping them build academic, social, and emotional skills to thrive. Engaging them with relevant problems that impact the real world. On the other hand, we have an eye to the future. We are shaping the generations that will shape the world. It's a humbling job. Our call to you is to embrace the challenge! Create authentic, meaningful learning opportunities for kids to help them be the best versions of themselves *today* so that they can go on and give us the best version of our world *tomorrow*.

References

Edmonson, A. (2012). *Teaming: How organizations learn, innovate, and compete in the knowledge economy.* Jossey-Bass.

Graham, P. (2005). *Schooling America: How the public schools meet the nation's changing needs.* Oxford University Press.

National Commission on Excellence in Education. (1983). *A nation at risk: The imperative for educational reform.* The National Commission on Excellence in Education.

WMA - The World Medical Association-WMA Declaration of Geneva. (1948). WMA - the World Medical Association-WMA Declaration of Geneva. https://www.wma.net/policies-post/wma-declaration-of-geneva/